The P.A.C.E. Method:
CONFLICT RESOLUTION for First Responders

Handing the Public & Working With
Fellow Professionals In Times of Crisis
POLICE EDITION

Mary Kendall Hope, Ph.D., with Director Richard Brewer,
BLET, DOCC Academy Training

Pax Pugna Publishing
Raleigh, North Carolina

Pax Pugna Publishing
An imprint of LuLu Press
3101 Hillsborough Street
Raleigh, North Carolina 27607

ISBN: 978-1-312-68492-8

Printed in the United States of America
Book Design: Mary Kendall Hope

Co-Author:
Richard Brewer, BLET Director, DOCC Director, Guilford County, North Carolina
Basic Law Enforcement Training, and Director of Detention Officers Certification Courses.

Specific Law Enforcement training details and guidance provided by Richard Brewer, Police Academy Director and trainer of all academy programs. Director Brewer is a veteran of over 40 years of professional law enforcement service and training. He is a retired Police Lieutenant with 15 years experience as an instructor of contemporary police protocols.

Special consideration is given to the support of **Fire Captain, Denita Lynch**. Captain Lynch is a Fire Service & BLS (Basic Life Support) Instructor and Level III Fire Inspector. A veteran of twenty-five years of Fire/EMS Service, her input assisted me with predominant fire protocols and procedures needed for instruction & training.

Contents

Acknowledgements

I would like to dedicate this book to The Heroic
First Responders in the U.S.& In Countries Throughout Our World
Thank You for Being There to Save ALL of Our 'Bacons' When
We Need You The Most
I Would Further Like to Acknowledge
The Inspiration and Support of
Dr. Arthur Slatkin, Police Negotiator, Author & Counselor
To:
Senior Officer Jason P. Lurz
And The Greensboro Police Department
Thank You for Allowing Me to Ride Along & For Helping Me Make
This Manual & Workbook
More Focused on Often Unique The Situations Police Professionals Experience
To:
Captain Denita Lynch
High Point Fire Department
Thank You for Helping Me Make This Manual & Workbook More
Specific to Fire & EMS Response
For:
Dr. Macgregor Frank, Director of the FIT Program
Guilford Technical Community College
I Would Like to Express My Appreciation
For Your Support
And Caring of My Work as a Trainer, Teacher and Writer
During my Time There as An Instructor.
For:
The University of North Carolina at Greensboro's
New Peace & Conflict Studies Department
Thank You
For Your Support of My Work To Establish New Theory & Training Techniques
To:
The **Guilford County EMS Professional Staff**
Thank You For Allowing Me to Ride-Along
& Experience Emergency Response First Hand
To:
Director Richard Brewer
Thank you for your invaluable Feedback & Advisement
Without Your Input & Support,
This Books Would Not Have Been Possible

Chapter 1

Five Phases of Conflict Resolution:
The Missing Link in the Chain

The RING of First Response

I present this training to you from a background as a *Second Responder* (crisis counselor). I would also classify doctors, social workers, nurses and other community service provides as potential second responders. I obtained my master's in counseling in 1995, and began seeing members of the public that year. Today, I am primarily an instructor and writer in the field of conflict resolution. Earlier this year, I published a new book for our academic field of conflict resolution and I included the work of police officers as the first axis in the phases of conflict resolution.

Police officers come into a crisis or conflict situation the <u>Scene MANAGEMENT</u> or **Intervention** Phase (below). A Crisis has just happened and professionals are called in to manage and stabilize the police call or critical incident – which could be *man-made* **or** *nature-driven* crisis (hurricane, tornado, flood, fire, or other force of nature).

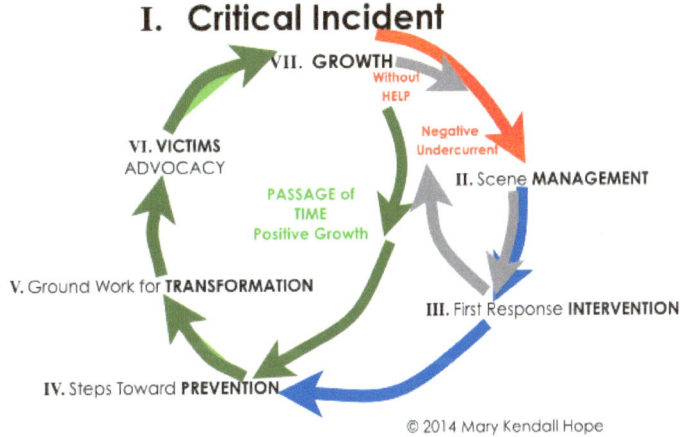

© 2014 Mary Kendall Hope

Man-Made Crisis – is a conflict or crisis situation that has been created by a person or persons. It usually stems from an existing conflict or crime in progress. **Nature – Driven Crisis/Conflict or Catastrophe** – was initiated by a force of nature. Floods, Tornados, Hurricanes, Nature-Created Fires, Disasters or Medical Emergencies fall under this classification. Once a situation is stabilized it becomes important HOW/WHAT initiated the emergency for real-time analysis and future analysis and understanding of the effectiveness and vulnerabilities of protocols utilized.

Conflict Intervention - The use of a professional (trained in conflict resolution) or diplomat, first responder, counselor or other credentialed practitioner to provide skilled help to individuals in crisis or conflict. Corresponding to the *RING of FIRST RESPONSE* – Intervention includes Phases I, II, & III. In Phase I, Police officers are on the Scene from the inception of the Crisis – and thereby have the opportunity to effect positive change from the beginning. Scene MANAGEMENT & First Response INTERVENTION. **If first responders fail to connect the link(s) between crisis management and continued intervention, the missing links in the chain cause the cycle of violence to repeat.**

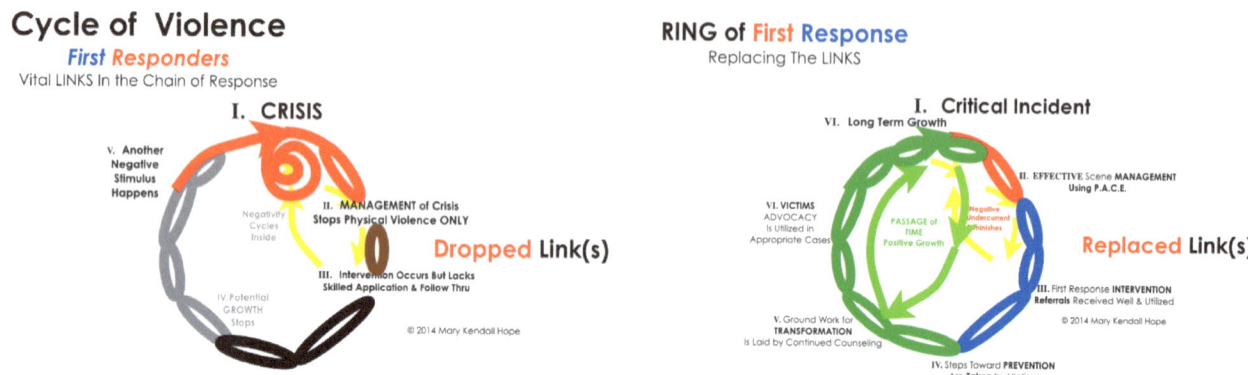

Conflict Prevention – The application of specially selected educational, diplomatic, and counseling resources to assist individuals to effectively understand and address conflicts positively. The goal of prevention is - learning better states of existence outside of prior conflict situations. Police officers here may not only connect victims to assistance, but also give pamphlets about domestic violence or other available community resources. In the *RING of FIRST RESPONSE*, the excellent work done by police officers to go the distance and assure victims are connected with help constitute phases IV & V – Steps Toward Solidified PREVENTION Education and Counseling & laying the Ground Work for TRANSFORMATION.

Transformation - A change in a prior state of being, going from a weakened, oppressed, and/or negative status to a better more positive state of existence - evidenced in a sustained set of positive interactions.

As Police officers, your excellent work to Set The P.A.C.E. makes THAT much difference in the lives of those you serve. How do I know? As a Second Responder of many years, I have heard this over and over first hand from those who have come into contact with both Poor Intervention and First Response AND I have seen how much difference it makes when a First Responder takes the time to do an Excellent Job by caring, showing compassion and going the distance.

WITHOUT Good First Response Interveners – Here's What Happens:

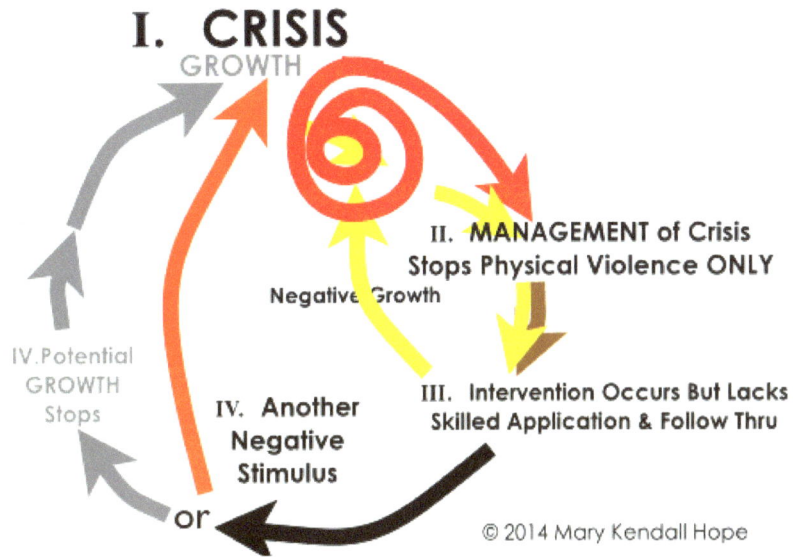

Cycle of Violence
Critical Incident

I. CRISIS
GROWTH

II. MANAGEMENT of Crisis
Stops Physical Violence ONLY

Negative Growth

III. Intervention Occurs But Lacks
Skilled Application & Follow Thru

IV. Potential
GROWTH
Stops

IV. Another
Negative
Stimulus

or

© 2014 Mary Kendall Hope

Cycle of Violence

    I customized this graphic to be applied to a critical incident, because in my theory of cycle of violence – all crisis stems from an originating critical incident (*from the perspective of the victim*). Sometimes, the incident may seem small and inconsequential in the moment it happens, but as time passes, the reaction the critical incident elicits *expands*. A first responder usually encounters individuals during a critical incident. The behavioral manifestations observed by first responders are often the first signs that a cycle of violence (that has been building) has worsened. Critical incidents can begin in a few badly held conversations or arguments – that usually stem from a simultaneous collection of poor interactions between two or more people.

    Sometimes, a cycle of violence begins (*first responder experience of it*) as a well-formed **large** entity. When the cycle is large, it is easy to fit just about any crisis call into the imagery above. ***Poor First Response*** stops the physical violence only in phase II. Interveners show up to the critical incident, but *without* the skill that The P.A.C.E. Method provides. A lack of skilled intervention deadens the conflict in Phase III, but soon, another negative stimulus propels the conflict right back into crisis again. The potential for recovery, healing, and growth is lost, creating a warped ellipsis (*orange internal arrow becomes outer rim of ellipsis*) that wobbles back into crisis repeatedly.

5 Stages of Conflict Resolution – The Professional *Address* of Each

This table depicts a description of how the field of Conflict Resolution categorizes the stages of conflict and conflict resolution – within the larger scope of **mass critical incident** conflicts & crisis. These general concepts do apply on a smaller scale to every day 9-1-1 calls/crisis situations as well, because all have the potential to develop into a worse crisis – or recover and transform in long term healing.

---

5 Stages of a Conflict

I. **Crisis** (Natural Disaster, Severe Argument or Fight, Battle/Terrorist Strike & Its Aftermath/On-Going Fighting)

II. **Conflict Management** (Compartmentalizing Crisises, Prioritizing Sections of Conflict to Handle First – Through Defense (military or emergency responders) or Police Presence if necessary, Cease Fire Agreement, Peace Treaty or Negotiation, & Diplomacy,)

III. **Conflict Intervention** (Negotiation, Mediation, Facilitation, Arbitration, Advocacy, Medical Intervention, Counseling, Red-Cross Intervention - Began After Conflict is Under Control)

IV. **Conflict Prevention** (Education, Training of Professional Staff, Private Classes for Couples, Families or Groups, On-Going Private Counseling, Diplomacy, Nation Building, Investment in Communities)

V. **Conflict Transformation** (Truth & Reconciliation Commissions, Transformative Mediation or Facilitation, Private Group Counseling *Follow Through*, Follow up Facilitation or Meetings)

I. **Crisis** is how a conflict is first seen. The initial presentation of crisis is usually violent. If a professional researches an initial crisis *historically* he will find a significant stimulating set of events that spurn the crisis.
Every conflict has an origin in some form of crisis. The steps described next (II – IV) may or may not have occurred *after* the initial crisis. Individuals involved in a crisis may not have been aware that a crisis was occurring, and may only realize that they have been experiencing a conflict until much later. Delayed reactions to crisis are common.

II. **Steps to Manage** a conflict include all diplomatic, police, emergency or military actions taken to protect all individuals in a crisis from further harm.

III. **Interventions** in a conflict include all measures to provide professional skilled assistance from certified or qualified conflict resolution professionals that would help individuals involved understand and more effectively deal with the conflict or crisis that they have experienced. Professionals involved may include first responders, mediators, negotiators, diplomats, counselors, arbitrators, facilitators, advocates, social workers, Red Cross workers, medical professionals, or other community officials.

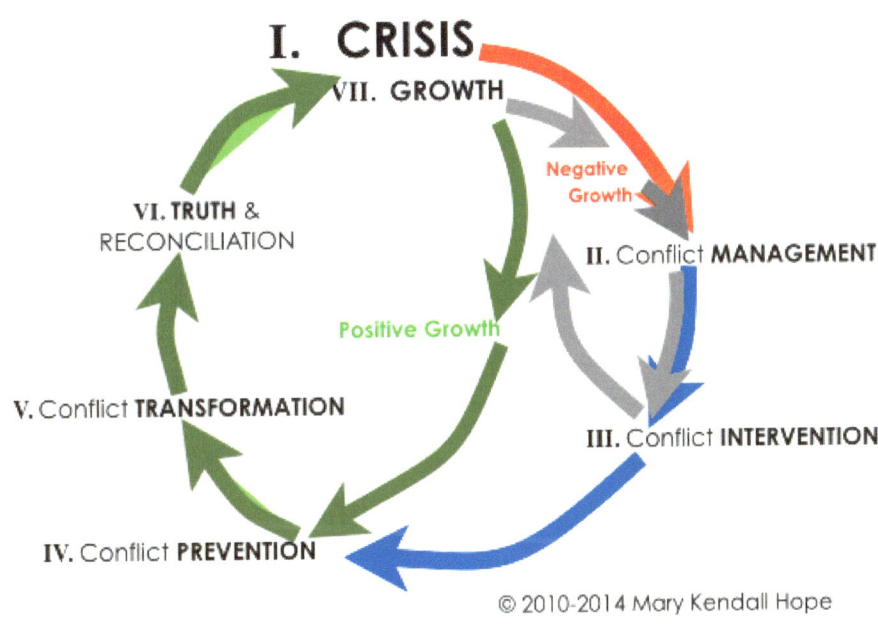

RING of Conflict Resolution
Encircling a Cycle of Violence

© 2010-2014 Mary Kendall Hope

IV. **Prevention** measures in a conflict situation include all education, planning, re-building, and on-going methods of counseling and intervention that are specifically designed to assist individuals to avoid another conflict similar to the one they have experienced.

V. **Transformation** of a crisis/conflict can begin in the intervention phase, but most often occurs after a considerable amount of time has passed since the initial crisis. The key element in transformation is time. Humans need time to absorb the shock from the crisis and consider the change in their lives that the crisis may have initiated or continue to initiate. Transformation is a recovery stage from conflict and does not always occur. Some individuals may never allow themselves to be positively transformed from a conflict due to past emotional pain that has built in their lives that can complicate the reactions experienced following a conflict.

Resolving Past Conflicts of All Types

Often, these steps following a crisis/conflict do *not* proceed in order and may break down and cease to progress (from management to intervention). Often, conflict stages can **end** either before or during the intervention stage and may *not* progress to prevention or transformation due to lack of awareness, endurance, emotional stability, energy, ability, skill to implement, or economic resources to continue to address a conflict. If the process to resolve a crisis/conflict breaks down, the conflict can still be addressed through the steps II - V, at a later date.

If a first responder seeks to intervene in an historical conflict that did *not* receive prior intervention or received poor intervention, then the first responder must understand that the conflict must be researched back to its original crisis stage I, to obtain a full understanding of how the conflict happened – what stimulated it and motivated the behavior to maintain it. For example: A police department is called repeatedly by one household – who subsequently calls the majors office on a regular basis. The chief decides to analyze this situation for the best address of the problem. The first step would include obtaining a thorough understanding of what *initiated* the original crisis. The effective address of such a crisis (repeated calls to police) would likely involve the professional assistance of other first or "second" response agencies – such as counselors, social workers, or other medical/professional help.

You as a *First Responder* may not become involved in these other stages of conflict resolution. In MOST of the critical incidents that you respond to your work to effectively interact with other professionals will stimulate a RING of Conflict Resolution that will better surround the problem. It is likely that several times during the course of your career, you will be faced with situations of mass critical incident or repeat crisis calls that will require the teamwork of multiple conflict resolution professionals to effectively address the problem(s). When this happens this book will provide you some background in conflict resolution. You will better understand how professionals can coordinate skilled intervention.

Chapter 2

*Be a yardstick of quality. Some people aren't used to
an environment where excellence is expected.*

Steve Jobs

Creating the P.A.C.E.: Police Calls & Critical Incidents
Let the Circle Be Unbroken

The **P.A.C.E.** (**P**reparing to **A**ct with **C**onsistency and **E**fficiency) is a concept created to assist police officers with conflict resolution skills. These skills will apply in both police calls and critical incidents such as: domestic calls, multiple car accident scenes; hostage/negotiation/ SWAT incidents; hurricane/tsunami response; tornados; local and national incidents of terror; floods; earthquakes; mass fire situations; and any other mass incidents of crime or crisis that affect multiple persons and geographic areas.

When any one of these situations occur, the police officers on the scene(s) are faced with a wide range of simultaneous challenges that require crisis scene management. Certainly, existing crisis intervention training has been a wonderful preparation for police officers in these situations. It is time to add to existing protocols.

The field of conflict resolution can provide another element of training for professionals who respond to mass crisis to assist in both the management of concurrent on-site professionals and the implementation of better protocols for addressing crisis. The PACE Method is designed to assist first responders; political leaders; medical and psychological professionals; and community leaders to coordinate professional efforts to more efficiently prioritize and address problems within a present crisis.

To **prepare to act with consistency and efficiency**, transforms an already highly skilled police officer into a professional who is ready to respond **verbally** to humans in crisis. The professional is further better prepared to assemble a team of assistance to surround victims of a crisis with the *best* immediate care available and assure victims are referred to on-going, and follow-up care. To assure referrals to second responders are accurate provides a better address of crisis and on-going conflict that can stimulate humans to recover *well* from a critical incident, instead of growing worse. The goal is for the RING or Circle of Resolution (surrounding the crisis) to be unbroken.

From a Conflict Resolution Professional's Perspective

As a conflict resolution writer, instructor and professional, I have forged a path from a jungle of unknowns since I came into the academic field of conflict resolution in 1999. I came to the field from a background as a successful licensed counselor, and I had been mediating disputes professionally in the business setting for a few years.

Helping individuals and families through some of the worst situations that they had ever faced prepared me for helping you as a first responder better verbalize and utilize conflict resolution skills to help individuals in crisis Police officers *each* have his/her own specific set of skills that are needed in times of crisis. You, as police officer decided to follow your own specific career because you felt you could really make a difference in the lives of those you would serve. You didn't choose this profession for a high paycheck, but rather to make a difference. I *share* this sentiment with you. And I hope what I have to share with you *here* helps not only you but also all individuals that you will touch. First responders need a very streamlined approach to service delivery. Therefore, I am condensing my educational instruction for you into a streamlined presentation specifically for first responders:

Defining a Conflict

Conflicts change the world. Conflicts change *people* with every small, medium, and large occurrence in which a person is forced to stop and realize that he/she is in the middle of a dilemma. Whether minor, every-day, or mammoth conflict is an essential part of life. In fact, I would go so far to say that the ability to acquire a positive response to conflict is a requirement of a healthy life.

I teach my students of conflict resolution that *conflict* is the "flip side" of *growth*, and without growth, there is no life. So instead of approaching a definition of conflict as a *terrible thing* every time it comes round, I believe it best to **define conflict (in terms of first response) as drastic change of reality – either severe or moderate in nature.** Yes, the conflicts that come to the attention of police officers are often terrible in their inceptions. Often, lives are lost and severe pain and damage occurs that changes the course of many lives. I do not wish to diminish this reality in any way.

The Growth Within

Every conflict has growth embedded within it. This growth can be either positive or negative (*more on negative growth later in the book)*. No, you do not say to an individual in crisis "you're going to grow from this..." It is not the right time to do that.

What you *can* do is 1. **learn what to recognize in human *expressions*** and 2. **learn what to say** that will open pathways for positive growth in time. The growth embedded within terrible conflicts is usually hidden to all involved during the first moments that a crisis occurs. Victims need to focus on surviving the drastic change that has happened first. This is where YOU the first responder meet them.

When a first responder is called upon, it is because something *life changing* has happened and it is usually painful and/or it threatens the safety or survival of those involved. Your job is to help them survive and re-establish safety. With this book, **I am not going to train you to become therapists or social workers.** Those skills are best left o professionals trained and credentialed to work with humans needing sustained support. All humans need sustained support following a conflict. What I am going to share with you are skills to help you better respond in the moments and hours following a critical incident.

During a critical incident, the individuals involved *need* you to focus on safety and survival, but your words of support and guidance to them can lay the groundwork for a positive recovery – as opposed to an atmosphere for a downward spiral. Police officers do not create downward spirals, but your wise eyes on a situation can help prevent one. You only have 5 – 10 minutes to interact with this person (more on rare occasions). Make those 5 minutes count. If you use your P.A.C.E. Method training, you Reinforce the RING.

Will the Circle Be Unbroken

There are very few *minor* conflicts. They may appear minor at first but if left untouched, conflicts worsen. In my experience, most people avoid conflicts – either dealing with them and/or acknowledging that a conflict is present. So, left to fester, conflicts build into real crisis over time. The type of crisis that often *first* faces a "first responder," because **people have been conditioned to call 9-1-1.** *That is "OK"* Whereas, calling a "Counselor" evokes a negative "stigma" that they must be "crazy."

What we must deal with is *reality* not what it "should" be or what people "should" do. Because people don't call counselors for help, they call 9-1-1. So it is up to us first and second responders to help them. Have you ever heard the old gospel song – "Will the Circle Be Unbroken…" The song essentially gives up on life down here on earth – saying only when we die – will hope that we – humans - will be surrounding by God's Circle …"in the sky Lord in the sky." (Habershon & Gabriel, 1907).

I don't know about you, but I'm not ready to give up on us humans' ability to help one another. In my first draft of the RING of Conflict Resolution, the RING was the "Circle" of Conflict Resolution (Hope, 2010). My titling then came from the image of encircling those in conflict with good, effective help. I amended its title to avoid the religious comparisons that can often be contentious – because the concept here is pure and **non**-denominational. It is about humans caring about other humans and surrounding them in times of trouble, regardless of religious affiliation.

It is easy for me to call up my memory the image of the front doors to the counseling center I worked in opening and individuals and families walking in following car wrecks, home fires, domestic violence situations, medical emergencies, and youth crisis situations involving suicide attempts, drug overdoses, hurricanes…

When a door closes behind an individual and a licensed counselor sits on the other side of the room – privilege and confidentiality laws immediately apply. The states of crisis that came to me over the years as a counselor taught me a great deal about the power professionals have to help. How humans experience crisis and how they absorb what is said to them by professionals during the first moments and hours following a critical incident leaves a significant impression on each human and what choices he or she then makes.

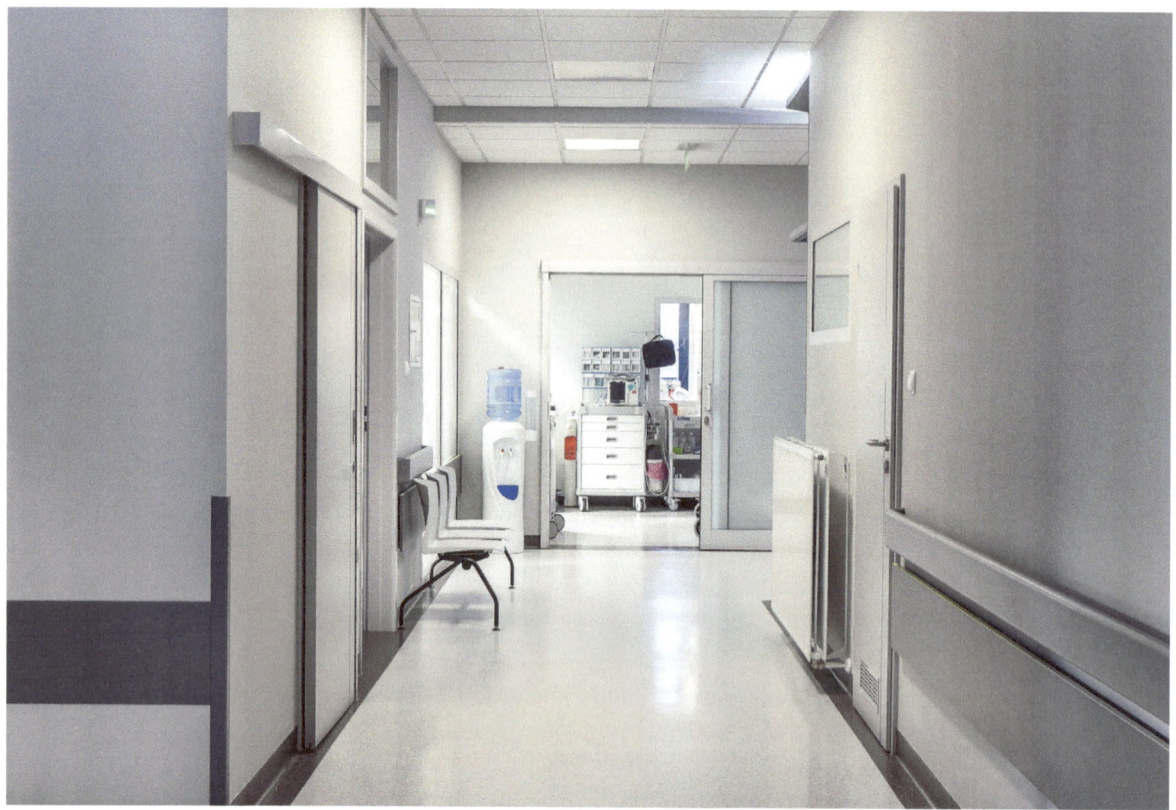

I created the PACE because training was needed as a simple guiding force to assist professionals when mass crisis strikes. Because I had been a "second" responder *myself* I knew that *focus* and *organization* were the tools the responder uses and these skill sets could be built on.

A First Responder (and the statements he/she makes to a victim) is arguably one of the most important aspects of an individual's ability to recover *positively* from a critical incident.

Earlier this year I published a new theory in my field of conflict resolution called "**Transcending Cycles of Violence.**" This is a text book for students of conflict resolution to help them to understand the "the big picture" perspective of how conflict resolution addresses the conflicts in our world – both internationally and on a small scale.

In that theory, a first responder constitutes the first link on the chain or using my analogy for conflict resolution students: "*RING of Conflict Resolution, Encircling a Cycle of Violence.*" If the first link is poor, non-existent, or weak, the rest of the chain fails, and the circle is indeed broken. In my experience this does not happen every time, but it does happen often. Often is too frequent. Rarely if ever is the goal. Remember, we all will need first responders OURSELVES at some time in our own lives. Do WE want the chain to drop when it matters to US or those we love?

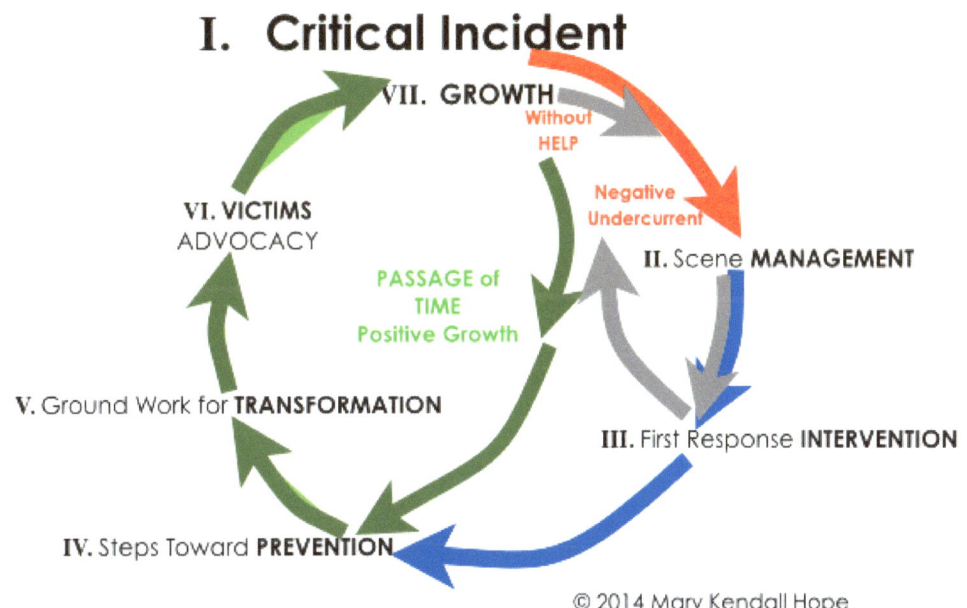

Every Time A First Responder Reinforces this RING – He/She **Creates The P.A.C.E.** and ROLE-MODELS for every *other* first responder and *every other situation* that comes after the way to handle this type of conflict. Every conflict is different. Therefore, EVERY time it is important to Do it Right.

PACE is a simple acronym that focuses the 4 most important concepts that *initiate* and *carry through* the process of responding to crisis and on-going conflict. <u>P</u>repare to <u>A</u>ct with <u>C</u>onsistency and <u>E</u>fficiency.

P repare to
A ct with
C onsistency and
E fficiency

This PACE is what both the *police officer* needs and what the *individual(s)* in crisis need from those who would help. The <u>Prepare</u> and <u>Act</u> portions of PACE make up the lion share of this training manual. **Preparation is always the most important and time-consuming part of any project**. The caliber of the preparation often translates into the difference between success and failure.

The Actions (this training manual provides) supplement your existing skill set with a new knowledge of conflict resolution techniques. **The Act(s) of:**

1. Listening/responding,

2. Comforting/Showing Compassion,

3. Referring, and

4. Following Through

with individuals in crisis constitute the conflict resolution skill I will share with you.
Your responses must be brief. - Therefore the need for a training to assist you to have these responses ready.

The one or two phrases that you will have time to make in a critical incident situation will make a positive difference **that will save lives in the future.**

The **Consistency** will be mastered by utilizing the companion book to this training of role-plays. Practice creates consistent responses. The **Efficiency** also comes with practice and with years of prior training and experience from your own respective professions. You've used the skills I have to share with you in other contexts. I am not bringing new flour, sugar or eggs to the mix – just a different recipe for using them in a critical incident.

Chapter 3

Opportunity is missed by everyone because its dressed in overalls and looks like work.

-- Thomas Edison

Introducing: The P.A.C.E. Method
Prepare to Act with Consistency & Efficiency

PREPARE

The best **Preparation** is the key to completing *any* task well. The more overwhelming the task, the more important preparation is to success.

Four essential components of good preparation for a first responder:

1. Completing your own certification/credentialing training with the very best of your own ability.
   Second best is not good enough for a *first* responder.
2. **Use The P.A.C.E. Method Training** with members of the public in crisis/conflict situations every time.
3. PRACTICE – Complete Role-Plays to Hone Your Knowledge & Ability to Deliver in 5-15 minutes
4. Recharge Your Batteries Daily (Stress Relief), Weekly (Weekend Rest), Quarterly (Get Away's), Yearly (Vacation)

Number one – your training – is a given, but essential. I'm not going to review what you've already been trained on. If it's been awhile since your training, assure you're keeping up with the best practices. Let me just ask you something, "**What do they call the Doctor who got a D- in medical school?**" DOCTOR.

Would you want the **D-** Doctor doing *your* surgery? If you got a D in any of your training courses – or even a C or B – go back and study some more. Did you get an A, **but you really don't *know* one part of it**? Know what you need to know extremely well. It will mean that *you* have a much *less* stressful job. It will mean that you will have a much more fulfilling job. It will save lives. It will mean that someone is hurt *less* and helped more.

Number two – The P.A.C.E. Method- you are reading this book – I hope you take it to heart and use it. I urge you to go through a P.A.C.E. Training with discussion and role-play work. In my experience as an instructor, students and professionals do **not** *l*earn without sharing in real-time in person discussion and role-play work with others.

Number three – PRACTICE – I must include here – I focus more on this in the consistency and efficiency sections, but if you don't practice, you will *not* be prepared and you won't realize any difference in your ability to respond to people better.

Number four is where the lion share of this Preparation Training benefits you.
Prepare *Yourself* First at Home.

Preparation to help *others* begins when the professional first shows up **prepared *internally*.**

Deal with your own demons. One's own state of calm is the most important skill *you* as the professional will bring to the scene. You know from your training as either an EMS, Police, Fire or other emergency worker that you should not go into this type of work if you have large unresolved issues of emergency in your own life.

If you haven't absorbed this aspect of prior training in your field before, please do so now. Emergency responders who themselves live in a state of emergency are *not* in the position of providing good assistance to others in crisis.

Recognize when you are in crisis or a deeper state of conflict in your own life.

Consider this scenario:

1. **Imagine** a time you came into work and it was a **bad day.** We've all had them, but a first responder has to have a place to put away a bad day. **First though, you must be able to recognize that you're not at your best and be able to be honest with yourself.** Stop expecting yourself to be perfect.

   - You have to deal with the issues that caused your bad day. Call the person you're in conflict with. Forgive them. Come back to the problem you have with them later and resolve it right. You will feel better and *be* better if you forgive them for being wrong (or you for being wrong). And give *your* best at work.

Answer these questions for yourself:

2. **Are you actively involved in a stressful career/live change?** This may include death, move, job change, divorce, caring for a family member who is ill... You will know instantly if this is your circumstances. If you are able to healthfully admit this to yourself, then good, you *can* deal with this well. **Take a support position only** in the mass crisis you are about to respond to. Take some time to deal with your life change well before placing yourself in a position of leadership. Return to leadership when you know you are ready.

3. **Are you actively hurt – either physically or psychologically? Psychological pain is important to give validation to.** Psychological pain is just as much a *physical* vulnerability and deserves time to heal. Again, take note of this and take a supportive role rather one of leadership. If you find this is not possible, do not lead beyond your physical stress level.

Address The Issues – Good Conflict Resolution At Home
Is a Job Requirement of a First Responder

There is no shame in having personal conflicts. If you didn't have them, you would not be human; you would be a computer chip. When you have a problem, be proactive in your personal life. Schedule a time with the person you are in conflict with to resolve the issue. Take them out to eat; talk later in private. Keep it simple. Simple works.

Even if someone has wronged you, be the bigger person. Let it go. Forgive them. Move on. As a first responder, you need to gently confront issues of conflict in your life and take the time you need to resolve them well. You cannot afford to live a stressed out life – it is a job requirement for you to be able to return to a state of calm and confidence. If you didn't take this away from your certification or credentialing training – take it away from *this* training. Police officers need to be the <u>best</u> a conflict resolution in their own lives, in order to be their best on the job.

Make no mistake. A first responder in crisis will inevitably spill his or her own crisis into the job. It will happen. You must *make* the time to deal with the stressors in your life. Make it a priority now.

Recharge Your Batteries

When I opened this section on preparation, I listed a "recharge batteries" daily, weekly, quarterly and yearly. That was NOT an ideal. If you haven't been taking time *every* day to work out and de-stress, it's time to.

Begin a new lifestyle of daily time to work off, talk through and release stress as a mandatory requirement equivalent to eating, sleep, water, oxygen...for these are the behaviors of a well-functioning first responder who is able to provide his or her best to others in crisis.

If you are a first responder, and you have not embraced a lifestyle that includes daily stress relievers, do so. Change your daily routine. Integrate an hour of stress relieving exercise on a daily basis.

A Second Responder's Experience in Daily Stress Relief

I will never forget my first job as a master's level counselor. I had a very small office that had truly served as a walk in storage *closet* before I was hired. It was cold and dark and there were no windows. The weekend I was hired, I came in when the building was closed and installed a small heater, two lamps, a soft set of chairs & pillows, and a large picture over my desk that simply stated, "Peace."

The next Monday, my schedule was full – eight separate individuals and families to see. People came in one after the other, hour after hour. I went home that day and began a routine that has not left me in the subsequent 19 years that have passed. The first thing I did when I got home was take a off the suit, shower and change into the "fun" clothing of my own personal life. I also found that a daily "run" (or exercise) served to release the stress of the many traumas that I absorbed each day.

I made up my mind in that first week that I had to train my mind to turn "off" its dwelling on these confidential traumas and think only of my life, my children, and my own goals of happiness, fulfillment, and personal challenge when I was at home. That strategy has served me well. I recommend this to you. Actually, what I have found as a professional, (observing others enter into the fields of police officers) is most do not make it if they do not begin a ritual of daily stress relief, rejuvenation, and personal prayer or meditation.

Belief in a Higher Power

As a second responder, I often sat listening and simultaneously praying in silent meditation for the person sitting with me. Hearing the pain of their stories and struggle is saddening, but over the many years I have practiced, I have learned that a focus on spirituality transfers a positive energy to me and helps me as a professional to deal with the traumas that I help others to face.

To have this sense of spirituality, one must regularly maintain a spiritual life. When I was actively practicing professional mediator and therapist, I began each day and evening literally on my knees in prayer to God to give me the right stimulus, the right words to say in comfort. As a writer, I do the same over every chapter and book I complete. A daily spiritual life (no matter what the denominational inspiration) or even just a deep sense of spiritually focused reflection is needed to do this job well, because the consequences to those who come to you for help are often serious and for first responder – sometimes the consequences are fatal.

Police officers are tasked with helping individuals deal with the ugliness of life that no one has answers for. What we represent as professionals in society is a group of individuals who seeks to guide those in *trouble* through the rough caverns of their crisis or conflict – toward a resolution that will both heal them in the long run, and stimulate a new growth in the present.

Weekly, Quarterly, Annually – Keep It Up

Carve out time every weekend to do nothing – just relax and enjoy the beauty of your family, friends, and life. If you don't, your daily work to relieve stress will soon fail to work – because a first responder needs a little more down time – even more than the average stressed out person. Quarterly = MAKE TIME to drive out of town. Save your "pizza money" or pack your lunch. Save the gas and "out to eat" money – and get a nice place to stay overnight and take a short quarterly trip. You need to get out of the town you live in periodically and see the rest of the state you live in. It will be good for your job. It helps give you a new perspective on every aspect of your life.

Don't skip an annual vacation. If it has to be a "stay-cation" for part of the week, then so be it, but it is best to actually take a vacation out of town. Do something that is challenging and fun. Learn something you always wanted to know how to do. These battery re-charges will pay you double when you return to work. You'll be more prepared to give your best.

PREPARING YOURSELF with these Four Priorities will:
- Focus you to **Ask the Right Questions**,
- Help you **Respond Well** with the best answers,
- You'll be able to **Recognize** when those in crisis are "Faking Good" and Need Your Support & Referral.
- You Will Know **When** need you **To Pull out your Pocket List**
- It will help you know **Who To Call/Refer**.

ACT

The next four priorities to guide your professional ACTions are listed in order of use. I will **begin with number four and number one** because number one – prioritizing your game plan begins with HOW you will deliver it.

1.   Prioritize Your Game Plan for Help and Follow-up
2.   Give yourself 15 minutes more & Other Professionals 30
3.   Assure You Know Before You Speak
4.   Deliver Actions With The 3 C's Confidence, Calm, and Compassion.
      Avoid the S & S- Stereotyping & Stigma

The Three C's – Confidence, Calm & Compassion

Having worked with a number of police officers, I have recognized that all police officers bring with them a calm and confidence in their affect. Most present a confidence and calm that can be a bit contrived – because it appears like it is simply part of the job requirement. I want to share with you right here and now that there is a big difference between calm and confidence that is *contrived* and the real thing and EVERYONE can recognize the difference.

Real compassion comes from the ability to listen and show the right amount of caring and it comes from a deep peace down inside. When you see a fellow citizen as *human*; when you take time to look him or her in the eye and truly listen to what this person has to say it significantly changes the situation. The ability to show compassion with confidence conveys wisdom.

Caring and compassion don't mean that you let people get away with things that they have done wrong. It means that you take the time to show your life experience and understanding. It doesn't make you any less of a man *or* any weaker as a female first responder to look someone directly in the eyes with caring and say:

"I understand. I would feel that way too." Here's what I need you to understand…" State it. If the person tries then to manipulate you, say: "Let me respectfully interrupt. I need to …..(return to my vehicle)….(complete this _____ job objective….)" You complete the sentence with respect. You then remove yourself to your vehicle or other place and formulate your priorities to help this person.

People respect strong, caring, professional help, even if they don't like it. If someone has to write ME a ticket, I may not like it, but if the first responder treats me with respect, I respect that person. Respect comes from compassion. **Compassion** is caring, empathy and understanding rolled into one. *I present a deeper discussion of the importance of empathy in chapter eight – mediation skills for the first responder.* **Empathy** means showing someone that you understand how he/she feels.

The S's in Crisis - Bring Out Our Stigmas & Stereotypes

It is simply how humans respond. We label what we do not understand – especially in times of crisis.

Check yourself for personal prejudice _honestly_. All adults form judgments. Professional responders must be honest about their own judgments before they can *drop* them and focus on objective to help all equally. None of us want to admit out loud that these feelings exist. They do.

That is why I feel the need to write about this reality here. I have seen it happen time and again. It is best to call yourself out and recognize the ugly truths of what you feel and believe and be prepared to face all of these predetermined judgments. In times of mass crisis, so many variables and types of individuals come at a first responder simultaneously that a professional often does not remember to check himself/herself in the moment.

Take Out the S & S

Never stereotype. Do not perpetuate stigma. Take time to listen to people without seeing color, clothes, culture…. I realize these aspects of a person's profile are important. I truly do. I did socio-histories on individuals for a living for many years. As a first responder, if you stereotype – you diminish your ability to truly help people. You won't see their needs. You'll see what you *think* they need.

There is an easy way to eliminate stereotyping – **Ask simple questions.** Do not assume; ask. **"What is the best help I can give you?"** Where? What Time? How will this___ specifically be best? Ask questions that stimulate one to two word responses. You'll likely get longer answers. Listen, Ask the specific question again. Help them focus.

Open your mind. Consider carefully what you are hearing. Change what you may have walked into a situation assuming. If you take out the S, you'll double or triple your ability to assist this person to resolve this situation. Take out the other S by recognizing when others in a crisis are perpetuating a "stigma" on those who are vulnerable and stop it by leading. Support those who are vulnerable by verbally saying "It's going to be okay. This is not your fault."

Number Two – Give Yourself 15 Minutes More Than You Think
You Need. Give A Fellow Professional 30 Minutes More.

Why? Giving yourself more time to carry something out relieves your own pressure and frees you to do your best job. It always takes longer than you think because you are working with other people – and other people are working off of a different agenda. It is just reality. Accept it.

Be patient and courteous, everything you do and act on will come out better if you allow people twice as much time as you think you need to do something. People are happy when it happens sooner, and if it takes that long or longer – they are not as upset. The last thing any first responder or victim needs in a critical incident situation is additional time pressure.

Number Three – Assure You Know Before You Speak

I cannot tell you how many times in the last few years that I have encounters both police officers and other professionals who told me something that they presented as fact – that was absolutely not. It was some version of "fake it till you make it," in my judgment. Fake it till you make it does not apply to police officers. Do NOT tell anyone anything until you KNOW you are stating fact.

You are making actions that change people's lives. It doesn't matter that *you* think you'll look foolish if you do not know. FIND OUT. Take a few minutes and find out where the person can get the best information. Do not tell people something that you have not verified. I know this sounds obvious, but I include this because I am seeing so many younger professionals do this. Your hard work to help people will be lost if you don't stop to verify the information you've given.

CONSISTENCY
1.   **Turn on Your Professionalism Daily**
2.   Bad Day – Take 5 To Re-Set
3.   Share only brief positive stories with members of the public.
4.   Homework- Find your **Compassionate** "Game Face" & positive attitude and put it on every day every time like your second invisible shirt.

Number one – Be the same reliable professional every day

To reinforce your existing training – you're a first responder. You've signed up for a job whose first objective is reliability. Reliability begins on the inside. You find the professional inside first, so that when the uniform goes on, it goes on with a good feeling every single time you wear it.

The P.A.C.E. Method consistency comes from practice – but it is developed when you have your **Number two -** first bad day.

You thought when you left home you had *dealt* with it. You hit the job, and you realize, *I just feel rotten.* I'm tired, mad, sad, frustrated….

STOP. You're human. You're intelligent enough to recognize when you feel bad. Give yourself a break. Take a few minutes and get a beverage. Have a meeting with yourself.

If it's exhaustion, the answer is caffeine during THIS day and some extra time from something *else* you needed to do – to REST. Re-book the something else you wanted to do tonight and get some rest or medicine. I know this seems so simple. **So many police officers get into a pattern and it's hard for them to break it.** One of my uncles was this way – *God Rest His Soul*. He had two speeds – HIGH and OFF. In his case, off came quickly in an accident he was too tired to see coming.

Number three - if you feel you must share your own personal experience with a member of the public or co-worker, it is best if you tell someone a similar experience that you have dealt with *well*. Sharing <u>bad</u> feelings will not help you or the situation. Dealing with bad outside of work helps you to present a consistently genuine professional – ready to give the best of himself/herself. Go back to "prepare yourself section." If you feel that sharing a few brief words will help - assure the key concepts are brief and positive – and you only share *successful* resolutions. Your knowledge of how a conflict was positively resolved will help those in crisis. Of course, your best skill is to be a good listener.

Number four – Practice Your COMPASSIONATE Responses

Wear your compassionate game face like a piece of your uniform. It's your new invisible shirt. You can do it. Get out a mirror and really take a look at what the public sees when they see you. I recommend making a video of yourself. You will learn a lot about how you present yourself to others. You want people to immediately see your confidence, calm and compassion CONSISTENTLY. To do this – work on it.

Practice the following statements:

" I understand how you could feel that way."
"Here's what we need to do…"
"This professional can help you beyond today to get through this better."
"Allow me a moment, I will find out where you can get that information."
"Let me interrupt you a moment. I understand. I need to complete this____."

EFFICIENCY

Efficiency comes from both continued accurate knowledge and practice. ***Debrief*** after a critical incident that involved multiple deaths, injuries or extreme traumas to both members of the public & police officers.

1. **Sharpen the Blade** –if your department isn't taking time to Debrief, or do Role-Plays to stay fresh – Suggest it.
2. **Re-write the script.** Even if you've done it wrong a hundred times. STOP. Do it right from now on. Re-write and rememorize a NEW script. A better way will be better for YOU, Your Department, The public, and the profession. . Use the same compassion and adapt as needed for each crisis.

The *Role-Plays for Resolution II* Workbook that goes along with this book is designed to provide you the practice you will need to attain efficiency. Efficiency comes with practice. **There is no such thing as a short cut to efficiency for police officers.**

The P.A.C.E. Method

The P.A.C.E. Method has many of the same elements and steps as your existing crisis training. I like to compare the difference between this training and existing protocols to **the few steps between first class and coach on an Airplane.** Both first class and coach have seats and refreshments. But the differences between the two experiences constitute some very important differences in the experience of the flight on this plane – at least that's what people on the plane would tell you. They're right of course. **The steps between the two are a very important few steps.** A critical incident experienced with police officers *without* The P.A.C.E. Method training is different as well.

The **consequences** of the critical incident last a lifetime.

Chapter 4

Facing the Scene:
A Fresh Crisis Needing Management

Police officers in the United States receive excellent training and have my deepest respect and support. I have lived under the benefit of that support throughout my life. The reputation you have, you have *earned* through fire, often literally.

I defined my background in chapter one as essentially a *second* responder (crisis counselor). Here's what a second responder can teach a first responder about a fresh crisis scene needing management: As you secure that scene, remember, **a victim's first steps out of quick sand mean very little if they slip right back in deeper after you've left them**. In slipping back in, humans usually grasp on to others and pull them down as well.

As a first responder, don't just pull them from danger and say:

First Responder	Individual In Denial
"Ok, so you're good?"	Yes
"Would ***this___*** help you to feel better about this?"	No
"Here's a pamphlet to help you"	No thanks. I can do it.

Physical safety and security from harm is the easy part. Psychological harm assessment is murky because you can't always tell when someone is lying to you. Sometimes, individuals don't know *themselves*. Denial is an invisible defense mechanism, in place to protect a person from psychological pain. It is painful and embarrassing to admit that one is weak and in need of *even more* help. This is true of everyone.

Victims of either a *man-made* or *nature driven* crisis are already in a state of vulnerability and humiliation because their lives are upside down. No one wants to find himself/herself in such a situation. **To experience a crisis and *next* have to admit that you need counseling or additional help takes a courage that most humans do not possess in the moment a critical incident happens.**

As a first responder, it is now your job to know this:

❖ Victims of a critical incident <u>ALL</u> need support after their physical safety has been re-established.

What Critical Incidents & Flu Viruses Have In Common

When a person experiences a critical incident it is like catching an air-borne virus (which also can be a medical critical incident). You need medical treatment (emergency response) to recover, but to heal you need to take care of your body so that it can fully recover.

Viruses are parasites that stay with you – so too is true of the stimulus and consequences of a critical incident. To heal from a critical incident, counseling is needed. Counseling is the Vitamin C of critical incident recovery. Vitamin C helps the body recover from a cold virus. When applied in advance, it prevents the cold virus symptoms or lessens the effects of another cold. The same is true of counseling. **One of the best gifts you can give to anyone - going through a critical incident - is to remove the stigma of going to counseling.** Tell them outright – Counseling is like going to the doctor when you have the flu. It's the right thing to do and it will help you feel better, get better and keep moving forward *positively* in your life. Here's what it would look like:

First Responder	Individual Listening
"The scene is now secure. Here's a couple of referrals many folks find helpful:"	**Ok**
"This is a person & his number that I know will answer and who specializes in _this_."	**Ok**
"What you've been through is stressful. I recommend – that _this professional_ can continue to help "	**Ok**

Individuals in crisis **_need_** a first responder to say this to them. They are afraid. Their world is likely in chaos. A critical incident makes everyone feel vulnerable. If they've gone through a critical incident, they have just been embarrassed and they feel humiliated, afraid, weak, maybe angry, sad, frustrated... the <u>last</u> thing they want or need to feel is stigmatized as "*in need of mental help* or in need of *a referral to social resources*"

When a professional person **refers a person to counseling,** he/she automatically feel like- **_they think something is wrong with me._** This is because society has repeatedly reinforced this stupidity in TV shows and movies for the sake of a cheap laugh. **As a first responder, do not perpetuate this ridiculous stereotype.** Tell people that it is **good** to go to counseling. Going to counseling doesn't mean that you're crazy; it means that you're **wise.**

New Skills At The Scene

Two teenage friends of mine from the early 1980's became first responders. One became a volunteer fireman. One became a policeman. My friend who became a fireman told me one weekend that instead of going out us; he was going to "fire school." *Fire school*, said I, *what in the world is that?*

"*I* know," said my friend who was planning on going to the police academy. "They go to training like policemen do – to do a better job."

Police officers have been improving their abilities to respond to critical incidents throughout my lifetime. In the 1980's, **_conflict resolution_** wasn't a coined phrase or widely known concept. When fire, police and EMS workers were called, they showed up and did their best to save lives. Today skilled training has been monumentally improved.

Police officers understand the difference between a "**crisis**" which requires immediate attention to stabilize and "**conflict**" which requires on-going help to stabilize. Police officers are called to *both* types of situations because very often, humans dial 9-1-1 when they do not know what else to do.

When a *What To Do Guide* DOESN'T EXIST

One of the definitions of a conflict is – it is something that – a "what to do" list doesn't exist. Police officers know this better than anyone. So, what do you do when there is a problem and there IS NO immediate solution or option? Securing the scene has already taken time, energy and resources. Police officers are allocated only so much of all of these.

When you arrived on the scene you found BOTH – a situation you've dealt with *before* (that you applied your training and knowledge to) AND a set of variables you did not know what to do with - OR YOU SHELVED IT - for someone *else* to handle.

When you're faced with one of these two situations as a first responder, you can do one of two things (that have been done repeatedly by police officers in the past).

How many times has this happened to you? I would hazard to say that if you were honest, it happens more often than you want to think about. **Let's delve into the shelf. First of all, which things do you shelve?**

1. Domestic Disputes & Conflicts
2. Un-explained Psychological Behavior

These are the two types of issues I can help you to address with a couple of excellent response options before you take *the road more traveled by.*

THE OLD ROAD – MORE TRAVELED BY

OPTION 1: You say to *yourself* (and likely the person in conflict): "**I'm not the person to help you with that.**" This likely true (in that moment) and while it is best to be honest, the real problem comes NEXT.

You could simply hand them a pamphlet and phone number. While this is ultimately the right referral source, there is a better way to handle this. Take the time to refer them to the **right person & right phone number.**

Why? First of all, the number you hand them may connect to a phone tree *this* will not help them. Also, not knowing *who* to specifically ask for will leave them frustrated and they will likely give up. When you do need to refer someone for help – you need that phone number to be the right one and you need to refer them to a specific person who is still employed there and actively handling these types of cases well.

THE ROAD LESS TRAVELED BY – THE BEST SERVICE PROVISION

OPTION 2: "Let me see how I can help." And you go to your "ON THE SCENE " List that you keep in your pocket. I have included a template that can be photocopies in the Appendix, but here is a smaller sample:

ON THE SCENE Pocket LIST™
(Maintain the P.A.C.E)

©2014 Mary Kendall Hope

REFFERAL SOURCE	NAME(S)	PHONE
Counselors	_____	_____
Suicide or Other Hotline	_____	_____
Domestic Violence	_____	_____
Social Outreach Programs	_____	_____
Medical Clinic	_____	_____
Homeless Shelter	_____	_____
Food Pantry	_____	_____
Community Program	_____	_____
Red Cross	_____	_____
Salvation Army	_____	_____
OTHER	_____	_____

This list may be downloaded from my website for free (www.negotiatethis.org) – so that support staff *or* each first responder can copy this word document into an existing system to adapt it for use with names and phone numbers typed in. Because you can save and amend it – as phone numbers and professionals change – amendments are easier.

It is vital to keep a list that is as accurate as possible. Also, give people phone numbers that are specific to real people not emails or websites.

Individuals in crisis need to talk to a real person. They also need to talk to someone who knows how to understand what they need and a professional who has the experience to respond with comforting help.

Keep the list small, to the point and pocket size – so that every first responder can carry a list in his/her pocket at all times.

Failure to Communicate – The Weakest Link in the Chain

What the world needs now from police officers are *more* professionals who find someone capable to refer individuals *to* and follow through to make sure that referral is a good one. Sometimes, you will have to take option 1. Let me encourage you of something right here. If it is best for the situation for you to pass it on then pass it on, BUT before you let it go, find someone to pass TO - who WILL be able to carry out OPTION 2.

If you don't, you've dropped the "chain" of help at the beginning. What individuals in crisis need most is help that will sustain through their recovery. No, you as a first responder will not be there after the crisis is over, but you can help connect them with solid help that will be.

I know this sounds simple. The longer I live, the more I realize the importance of recognizing when *simple* is hardest thing to do. **The best first step ensures a secure second and third step.** In this situation, to NOT find someone who is capable (before you pass it on) is "failing to communicate."

Going the extra mile is draining work. When you begin to take OPTION 2 it will really cause you to be exhausted at the end of your first days and weeks. I know. I lived this as a counselor. What I also learned is that it gets so much easier over time, and as a professional, I felt so much better about the quality of my work, when I did my very best. I didn't get paid much, but I went to sleep at night knowing I had done all I could and I knew I had really helped those I came into contact with. I also learned very quickly to begin a new routine to take care of *myself*, so that my batteries were recharged, and I would be ready. *More about this in the next chapter*.

What to Say *Differently* ON THE SCENE:

Going farther down "the road less traveled," (Peck, 1998), I will use my analogy from above. On the scene, the most important thing you can do to help individuals in crisis is to de-stigmatize the social taboo of going to counseling and of getting help. Victims do not need "de-stigma" help with calling the Red Cross because this social program – as well as other we already know – are accepted by society as "ok." Calling a counselor is another story. We all know that everyone associates "going to counseling" with "being crazy" upon first referral. So refer them like this:

STATEMENTS I WOULD USE:

"If **I** were in this situation, **I** would call a counselor."
"**I** would go and talk to someone. It's the right thing to do."
"Counselors can really help you get help and get on with life."
"No one will know but you."
"Keep your private business private."
"Counselors can really help you get back on track."

The few words you say to be kind and supportive of counseling will make all the difference. A vulnerable person who really needs help is always afraid of the stigma of getting it.

Chapter 5

Setting The P.A.C.E.
The Moment You Step From Your Vehicle

Before you act, write, speak or step either from your vehicle or between one event and the other, stop. Breathe; refocus and remember your preparation steps.

SETTING the PACE

Both you and others will react based on how you present yourself. Set the PACE by becoming the calm, confident person you would want to see in your co-workers and in any person coming to see you in a time of crisis. *Your Reflection* -Remember your reflection in the mirror from chapter three? What are others about to see when they look at you? Assure your expression is one of confidence, calm, compassion and a 4th C - Can-Do attitude.

Before outlining the objectives to Setting The P.A.C.E., I would like to briefly present **the actions, which will *not* stimulate a positive experience**.

Often, interveners attempt to resolve conflicts without completely stopping to absorb the gravity of the perspectives of those involved and show respect of their present situation. A lack of respect of individual(s) *needs* and *perceptions* will ***not*** stimulate positive growth. **After you've stabilized the crisis - take the time to consider the perspectives of *each* individual before offering help.** Allow them to tell you what their needs are and validate their requests.

Individuals Not Groups – Do not Make The Situation Worse

Even though *groups* of people often experience major crisis and catastrophe, treat each person involved differently, according to the needs each person states. Even though the individual may show the same symptoms and characteristics as others you have seen in similar situations, do not lump individuals into "groups." This erases them as individual humans who have feelings and the potential to grow. Do not treat individuals like they are just part of a "whole" or mass who have experienced the same thing. Every time you do, you rob each person of empowerment.

When individuals feel like they are but "numbers" it lowers their self-worth and thereby their ability to transcend a violent situation. Remember it's *their* experience not *your* experience of helping that you need to focus on. If you are not able to make your own needs "secondary" consider going into a different line of work.

Remember your P.A.C.E. To place people in a square box because the stereotype fits for *you* does not help *them* at all. This may sound obvious, but the reality of my years of experience is that professionals do this all the time and are not aware of it. Check yourself, when you come to a place that you don't know how to proceed, stop.

Remember the ACT directive -Ask the person involved. If you don't you will hurt the situation and person more. This person (who has just experienced a crisis or violence) also has to overcome *your* prejudice as well.

Recognizing Individuals' Experiences

If a first responder walks into a post catastrophe situation and presents a nonchalant attitude of "I'm focused on what **I** need to do - you need to deal with *that* yourself." Reactions to new options for help will be not be received well. *Those you help have histories, and what they've been through is NOT known* to you, the first responder.

Sometimes, the only outside authority figures a victim of violence *sees* are police officers to a crisis. Therefore, the way the first professionals handle responses to violence and crisis are an important aspect of *not only* successful conflict management, but also the potential for stimulating this person to recover.

Stimulating Recovery– The First Steps

Approach any individual who is experiencing a crisis or violence first with empathy. Consider: How is this person feeling right now? Give them the benefit of the doubt and instead of expecting them to be strong enough to handle it, expect them to need your help, your caring, and your compassion. The responses a first responder gives to individuals experiencing violence, crisis, or extended conflict are very important because they form the foundation for whether these individuals will be able to grow and change positively.

Wasted Opportunities

Energy and time in these circumstances is very precious. **The opportunity to recognize one's need for help may not return for an individual in crisis, if he/she is not fortunate enough to experience good intervention** It may take years for this person to realize the need to find counseling again and maybe they never will. If you do not believe my theory and experience, look around you at the mass numbers of individuals who struggle to recover from critical incidents. From the moment you step from your vehicle, set the P.A.C.E.

Seven STEPS to Set The P.A.C.E.:

To stimulate positive growth once you've established a good rapport of caring and compassion with an individual, consider the following actions to Set The P.A.C.E.:

1. **Listen** to how the person feels right now

2. <u>Do not say</u> "You shouldn't feel that way." Each person has a right to feel angry, sad, afraid, frustrated and appreciates support. They will stop feeling that way in their own time and you will help them to feel better sooner if you let them feel bad first with consequences.

3. Do not attempt to provide an instant quick fix. Stimulate lasting healing by first taking time to really care.

4. Respond after listening with **"I understand how you feel. Though it's not my place to say who is right or wrong**, (when the person tries to "recruit" your alliance) …**Anyone would feel shock, sadness, frustration**…." Then stop speaking.

5. Continue listening. Do not interrupt. Allowing a person to talk de-escalates their feelings of crisis and enables them to feel empowerment from you

6. Have your counseling referral **POCKET List** ready and give them a number

7. Assure that the individual is referred to at least two or more resources before you leave them. Close the situation positively – more on this in chapter eight.

To respond to a person by listening with empathy, showing compassion, and telling this person that continued good counseling **will** help is the same difference as the distance between first class and coach. It's just a few steps, but they are steps that create an entirely different experience going forward.

Use Your 7 STEPS to P.A.C.E.
1. LISTEN w/Respect & Empathy
2. Don't "SHOULD" On Them
3. NO Quick FIX
4. "I can understand how you could feel that way."
5. Don't Interrupt
6. Use Your POCKET List of Referrals
7. Close the Situation Positively   ©2014 Mary Kendall Hope

Chapter 6

Failure is simply the opportunity to begin again, this time more intelligently.

Henry Ford

Why Do People Lose the Ability to *Reason*
In Crisis & What You Can Do About It

CRAZY

People act crazy when they are in crisis. No matter how sensitive you are to people or their circumstances, at least once (or maybe even multiple times) in your career you will find yourself describing victims as "crazy." Are they crazy? Temporarily, maybe so. In times of crisis, it is normal to act a *little* crazy (within legal parameters).

Mental health professionals use a diagnosis for this. It's called an "Adjustment Disorder." It is used to diagnose individuals who are continuing to experience problems adjusting to a post-crisis or critical incident situation. It is considered normal to experience symptoms of anxiety, depression and stress for up to six months following a crisis – depending of course upon the crisis and the severity of the actions, statements and overall general behavior of the person(s) involved.

If individuals act in a dangerous manner, this is an entirely different situation from both a mental health professional's perspective and a first responder's point of view. Knowing this, it is best to assume that victims are going to act "crazy" within an acceptable range.

WHAT POLICE OFFICERS CAN DO:

1. One of the best methods for dealing with individuals in a crisis situation who are not responding to reason is for you to **allow them to have a bit of a melt down in a safe place**. Don't judge. Remember, you or someone you love may experience the same set of feelings in this situation.

2. When others begin to *look*, question or try and intervene *poorly* – be proactive and use your P.A.C.E. Method Compassion – say: *"Please allow this person a moment to collect himself/herself"*

You do not have to say anything more profound or intellectually impressive. The small "break" you give someone who needs a moment can be the difference between someone being able to deal with this critical incident *well* or not.

It is best to keep an inexperienced first responder from dealing with a victim who is having a "melt down." It takes some years of life for any professional to know how to respond, and know that sometimes, to just allow a person time is best.

The less you say in the first moments, the better. The more you listen, the better.

3. Take a few moments once the person has calmed down and listen to them. Often, people in crisis who are acting "crazy" begin to immediately feel better when someone simply takes the time to listen.

4. You do not have to say very much to them. Just show compassion and when or if the person asks you for help – take out your pocket list and encourage them to use the referral you give them.

5. Tell them: ***"It's going to be ok."*** When a first responder takes the time to tell a victim this, it can immediately begin to help this person to feel like things will eventually be ok. In counseling, we call this empowerment.

6. Eliminate Persistent Problem Makers with respect and reassignment. Give them something to do that will help the situation.
   During a longer critical incident: **WATCH What they do over a 30-60 minute period of time**. If the person is acting like they are not in touch with reality – then send them for an assessment. To do this with respect provides the individual involved a better chance for acceptance of help by second responders.

7. Speak no evil – either to the person, the press or to a political figure. It will come back to haunt not only you but those who you are endeavoring to help. In fact, as a P.A.C.E. trained first responder, one of the best things you can do is speak only positively. It sets a role-model for all professionals who will talk about the critical incident.

PSYCHOTIC & SOCIOPATHIC BEHAVIOR

How do you know when "crazy" has just crossed the line into something dangerous? From your own training the "threat of harm" scale continues to be the first yardstick. Is this person claiming to harm himself or others? If so, take the person into custody. If he/she is *not* showing present threat of harm to self or others – how can you tell if there may still be good reason to take this person into custody – because they may be psychotic?

RED FLAGS – SECURE The Person & Call To Schedule Mental Health Evaluation

1. **Statements of Intent to Harm**. This is from your training, but do not overlook the obvious. Secure the person ASAP. Statements of harm – no matter how young the person – reflect a serious state of mind.

2. There is a **Written Letter** or posting on social media that states intent to harm or other threat, **statement of unusual intent that indicates that this person is not centered in reality**. Example: they are disassociating from personal relationships/work.

3. You've been **called by immediate family member(s)** who are <u>afraid</u> of this person. If you've been called by friends, co-workers, or community members: it is a red flag that needs to be verified, but **follow up and check the source.**

4. The person appears **NOT ORIENTED** to any one or more of these 4: **Time, Place, Person** or **Their Own Medical Condition.**

   a. **NON VERBAL Signals:** These you must see happening for a significant period of time or be significantly ODD in response to an automatic "norm" (within a wide rage) response:
      i. **VERY ODD Facial Expressions – Expressions on Face do not Match Words**
      ii. **Staring with Dilated Pupils into Other People' Eyes –Unexplained Movements**
      iii. **Seeing Images (hallucinations)… Dressed EXTRMELY inappropriately or Naked**
   b. **VERBAL Signals:** These will happen throughout your conversation <u>intermittently</u>.
      i. **Talk about Occurrences – UNRELATED to Critical Incident in Odd Manner**
      ii. **Not Responding Correctly to Questions=Giving Answers That Do not Make sense**

5. If they cannot give you a sound collection of responses *about the critical incident* that they have *just been through* – For instance – If this person has just experienced extreme violence and they are not appearing to understand what to do next, or they are ***talking about behavior that is unrelated to the critical incident*** in a manner that is **seriously concerning** because of the **long duration of time they have been talking** about something very odd or the subject matter itself…It's a red flag that they need to talk to a counselor.

These behavioral displays reveal that they actually *may* be in a state of temporary psychosis or may be sociopathic at this time. **It *may* be a temporary state. There also may be other reasons this person is acting this way.** The best thing to do is have this person talk to an assessment counselor – who in cooperation with a psychiatrist will be able to make an initial diagnosis and follow up with care to help this person recover in time.

OTHER TYPES OF "CRAZY"

Critical Incidents pull up the most extreme of all humans' emotions. Police officers are trained to react with professionalism, but crisis situations will inevitably bring up every person's past experience of fear, anxiety and failure. We deal with problems with the extent of the expertise we have – when that runs out – "the _____ often hits the fan" from both a first responder and a victim/perpetrator. Conflicts at the scene of a mass crisis or critical incident are common.

WHY DO POLICE OFFICERS HIT A WALL?

Because they do not stop and consider the entire problem. They only consider *their* perspective and they DISMISS the *other* perspective. This is a recipe for disaster and negative conflict.

⇒ When you think **"I am right"** and the other person is simply **"wrong" you will fail** in a conversation and ultimately fail within the circumstances that surround that critical incident.

⇒ Considering other people's feelings and perspective is the first step toward a good resolution. Good negotiation skills will lead to more success at resolving the bigger problem.

WHAT POLICE OFFICERS CAN DO:

Listen. Use Your P.A.C.E. Training to Negotiate *Well*

It is easy to fall back into old bad ways of *negotiating*, especially when one sees fictional movie characters and other *police officers* using bad negotiation skills. We all have moments of "crazy." We all appreciate it when other stop to care about us when we do. Extend this respect to the victims you encounter in a critical incident. It will de-escalate a situation that could get worse quick and spiral down into a worse experience. The next chapter provides more negotiation skills to help you when you must talk with a person experiencing mental health issues.

Chapter 7

Unfortunately, we force people to break the law in order to get any kind of mental health treatment.

Pete Earley
Crime Novelist

Dealing with Mental Health Issues
That Are Exacerbating the Problem

Dealing With Mental Health Issues

As a first responder you already know, you can't always just refer a person with mental health issues *instantly* to someone else. Sometimes, you must deal with them in the moment. If you don't know enough about what to do the crisis will escalate into something else that is more complicated. In these instances, I can recommend some specific strategies from my ***Negotiate: Resolve it Right*** book (Hope, 2014)

Negotiation is a job requirement for a First Responder – because in truth, you will negotiate every single interaction you have with a member of the public. For them it will be a critical incident. For *you* it is another day on the job requiring good negotiation skill.

Another truth I know is that negotiating *well* is a learned behavior. **When you begin to do it well, it becomes how you respond in other areas of your life.** It becomes how you speak and how you act. If you speak and act with disrespect, you will get disrespect in return from those you talk to. You will also worsen the conflict. Here's my adaptation of an old adage
as it pertains to Negotiation – Which is a Way of Life for a *First Responder*:

1. What one *thinks* becomes what one *says.*

2. What one *says* becomes what one *does.*

3. What one *does* becomes *habit* over time.
4. *Negative Habits Never Changed Make up a Life Choice.*
5. Habits Changed Positively, Change *Your* World Positively
6. All of the People in *Your* World will be affected by your habits either positively or negatively.

7. Choose Your Thoughts, Statements and Actions Wisely and with the Consideration of *All* Those Around You.

The way to deal with mental health issues – is the same as with normal issues – it just takes more patience to listen and MUCH more patience to Negotiate. Negotiating well is a process that begins *first* by understanding the **origins** of the conflict then **changing** the state of what isn't working.

⇒ Prepare to negotiate by going back to the drawing board and **be honest with yourself** about what you think *now* – and how can you **open your mind** to think about this in a different way.

WHAT YOU CAN DO - Learn To NEGOTIATE Well - - PREPARATION, PATIENCE & TENACITY

Every interaction in life is a negotiation.

Before we *ever* begin negotiating with family members, co-workers, bosses, authority figures, service people, salesmen.... we first negotiate with ourselves. We negotiate every word that will come out of our mouths and we negotiate every thought.

To know going into a potential negotiation that both you and the other person has something to lose and you both simultaneously have something to gain will empower you to find compromise. A negotiation is an exchange between what I want/need to happen and what the other person wants/needs to happen. Both can find common ground if both empathize with the other's perspective first – BEFORE beginning to negotiate.

Do not make assumptions.
Here's some questions to ask yourself instead:

THE OTHER SIDE'S PERSPECTIVE

1. What if you were in the other *side/person's* situation/position? **How would you feel?**
2. Would you be afraid? Yes.
3. Would you have negative feelings about *you* if you switched roles?

The *other* side has their own set of negative feelings – some about you, some about the entire situation as well. They have anger, sadness, frustration, fear, and a good reason for the way they feel.

You are not simply right and "they" are wrong. The *other* side is also not "right" and you are "wrong" either.

The truth always <u>Lives</u> *somewhere in the middle. The "truth" in my experience is a living entity that* <u>both</u> *must find together.*

❖ **I know this seems a fundamental truth that everyone surely understands as the basis of any argument, but what really happens to** <u>prevent</u> **people from negotiating is that they forget the simplicity and profound importance of this truth.**

People become blinded by their own fear that anyone will see their feelings as justified and they abandon their knowledge of the fundamental aspects of a conflict. They also fear that they will be able to successfully negotiate a resolution that will give justice to what they need and want.

From *Negotiate: Resolve it Right*: *10 Points to Successful Negotiation*: **The *Negotiate* Strategy™**

1. **Listen**
2. Respectfully **Make A Simple Request**
3. Do not argue. Do not justify your choices. Do not interrupt. **Listen**
4. As you Listen and **Consider What You Are Hearing**:
5. **Seek to Understand & Empathize** with the Other Sides' Perspective
6. Take Time to **Consider What You've Understood** Before Speaking Again
7. **Make Another Positive Statement** or Respectful Request

If the conversation isn't going well, stop and follow steps 8-10 without discussing points. If the conversation is now progressing well, continue slowly. Do not take on too much. Discuss only one point at a time.

8. **End the conversation after 1-3 points** have been successfully established or discussed.
9. **Close with statements of respect** and
10. **Thank the other side** for making time to talk with you. (Hope, 2014, p.6).

Your closing words should be something genuine and respectful, no matter what the other side has said. Leave the situation positively.

You can only control your own actions. No matter what the other side does, you will feel better if you do not engage in a negative statement or exchange.

Police officers - FACING The FEAR OF THE UNKNOWN

Facing the fear that *You* will fail to get respect and justice for your perspective is so hard that it is too difficult for most of us to accept at first. It is simply human nature. During a conflict a victim's first feelings are:

⇒ Anger, sadness, frustration...

To Help THEM Face The FEAR – **Name It, Do Not Be Ashamed of It**

Talk with the victim. **They need someone to just listen and care about their present circumstances for just five minutes**. – Do not tell them that they are right or you are right, just allow them to have a right to feel sad, angry and frustrated and not feel stupid for being human.

This doesn't mean that the victim is right about the entire set of issues. It means they have a point and have a right to have negative feelings. **Stop there.** It's not about getting them on your side or taking sides – it's about recognizing that this victim is afraid and being afraid is normal and healthy.

If a poisonous snake crawled in front of you – you'd be afraid. A conflict has just as much potential to "bite" this victim and permanently harm them. The fear anyone has of the snake can protect *them* if they act on this recognition wisely. **Help them act wisely.**

RESPONDING TO MASS CRISIS – Go The Distance

As a nation, we have seen *poor* address of mass crisis situations as reality in the aftermath of many large-scale critical incidents. The failures resultant from the Hurricane Katrina *response* came from poor diplomatic decisions, but also from nearly every type of first responder as well.

There were those police officers in that situation did a *good* job as well, but our failures to possess a protocol to handle a mass crisis incident continue to echo in regions throughout the United States. Though much was learned and improved since then, Hurricane Katrina aftermath could easily repeat itself in a different form.

Sometimes, when conflicts escalate it is because a first responder doesn't go the distance and contact someone who can and will help. Sometimes, it's because of inept professional responders. Sometimes, its because those in conflict are still raging and haven't been calmed down. Often, it is because police officers who deal *with* the conflict don't know what to do and let something drop.

What a first responder needs to know is **how to start a process** of *positive reaction* and healing. Without a beginning, a new story of recovery cannot be written. Police officers can be the spark plug that makes a "car engine of new health" run well again. Without the right set of spark plugs, the car simply doesn't go. Instead of throwing up your hands and saying "it's not my job," use The P.A.C.E. Method. Police officers Can be that spark that initiates a better resolution.

Vulnerability in Police officers – Will Victims Take Advantage?

Will victims potentially try and take advantage of your caring as a first responder? Some will. That's when your practice of your P.A.C.E. Method 3 C's No S comes back to PAY you. If you practice your confident responses, delivered with calm compassion and zero stereotyping, you will successfully negotiate the situation. Walk away confidently, calmly and without stereotyping the victim. They will get the message.

FEAR is Our Body's Way of Saying: "Stop, Think, Act Wisely."

⇒ The Victim/ Perpetrator, & You will be stronger if you **stop and allow yourself to relax and negotiate the situation well**. Once you've experienced this feeling of calm, the strength to face the *next* phase will come if you believe in yourself, and it will come more quickly and thoroughly than you ever knew possible.

WHAT YOU CAN DO:

Surround yourself with people who care about you and support your good work as a first responder. Spend more time with *them* than those who are *not able* to negotiate well. They will help you to feel and BE strong. Just like it is easier for a person on a diet to hang around healthy friends instead of their fast food eating friends – It will be better for you as a first responder to hang around with fellow professionals who use The P.A.C.E.– rather than those who allow their impulses to guide their actions.

Chapter 8

The Importance of Follow-Through
Closure & Follow-Up with Other Professional Agencies

A job is only completed when ***those who requested the job*** are truly taken care of and they say so.

Follow- Through

As a first responder your job requires you to be at the ready for the next call or crisis that comes at nearly any moment. EMS workers will need to accompany victims of medical injury to the hospital. Some Police &/or Fire Personnel may also be required to leave a critical incident to complete other duties. In these circumstances, back up police officers (Fire & Police Personnel) can be accessed to assure a critical incident scene is stable before leaving it. Remember our imagery from chapter five?

If you are presently working in a jurisdiction that does not practice this protocol (*of assuring that referrals are made to "second responders" when appropriate*) then I encourage you to amend this protocol to add this P.A.C.E. Method guideline. Good critical incident scene Follow-Through takes only a small amount of time – in comparison to the time spent managing the crisis.

If Police Officers Leave After Phase II – It's Coming Round Again

If all police officers simply leave the scene when the violence has stopped (and I've seen this as "normal" for many jurisdictions) then this situation is likely to repeat – and it will be worse next time around.

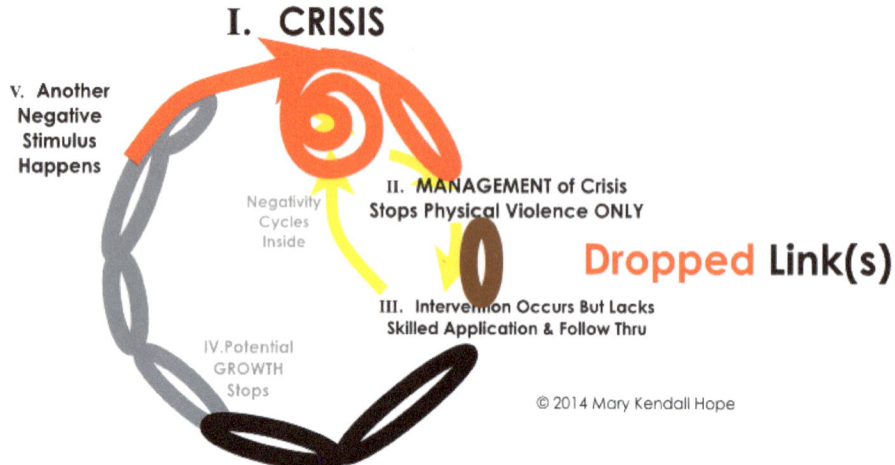

The Graphic above depicts the dropped link(s) in the chain that happen when first responders do not follow through. What you can do in just a few well skilled moments – using **The P.A.C.E. Method** can and will change a cycle of violence. Here is where the <u>C</u> – Consistency & <u>E</u> – Efficiency become most valuable. If you learn to use the preparation and action skills consistently, your efficiency at delivering the follow- through and closure that is needed will help you, your fellow police officers, community, and especially the victims of the critical incident to stop a cycle that is either repeating or beginning.

Without skilled intervention, victims of a critical incident will be lost. In turn, their loss will translate *out* into the community they live in as they "re-tell" the story of what happened. Other community members will also not feel confident in the professional help that they would call. Others will also not know how to prevent a similar critical incident response.

On the other hand, if you DO take the time to follow-through, assess closure and provide referrals – then you give victims of a critical incident help and hope. They will feel better. They will feel supported and empowered and you can do this as a first responder in a few well-skilled moments.

Encircling a Cycle of Violence - Transforming Into A RING of *First Response*

A First Responder Can Do This With 3 Important P.A.C.E. Steps:

1. **Assess the *Closure* Status** of the Individuals Involved
2. **Provide Basic Listening Skills** (3 C's & NO S or S)
3. **Refer Individuals** to the Appropriate Second Responders

Later, through your command structure protocol:

4. **Follow-Up with Other Agencies** To Improve Protocols & **Check Status** When Appropriate

RING of First Response
Replacing The LINKS

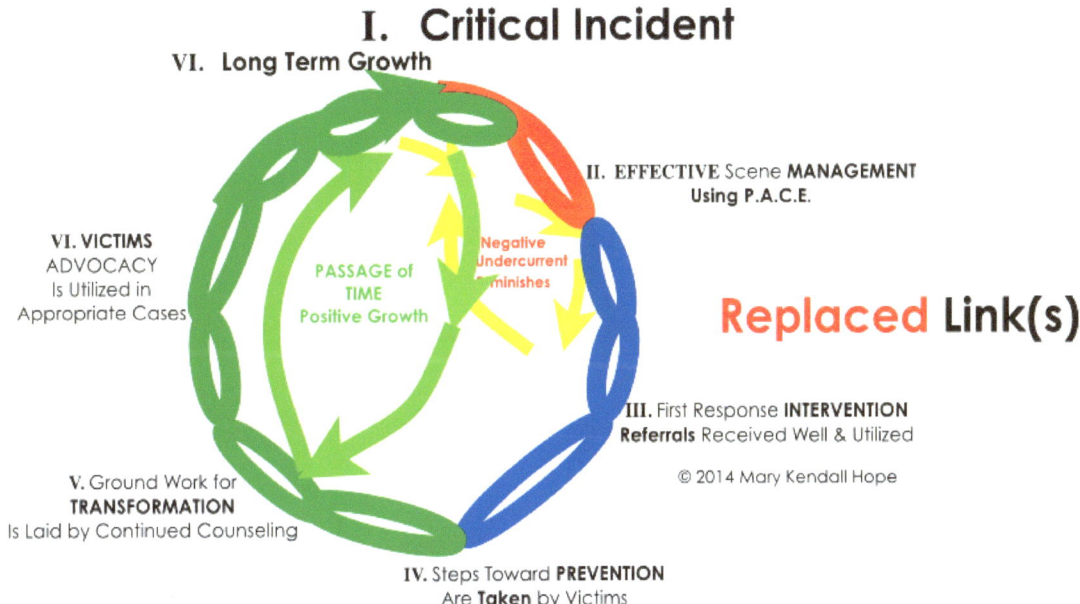

Completing these three steps will take your work as a first responder from Phase II Scene MANAGEMENT through Phase III First Response INTERVENTION and lay the groundwork for Phase IV PREVENTION. The difference between a first responder who just walks away and does nothing and a first responder who takes a few moments with victims makes ALL the difference. **It replaces the missing link(s) in the chain.**

The rest of this ring (IV-VIII) is handled by second and third responders, but **their link in this chain is not possible unless a few police officers first *begin* a process of support.**

1. Assessing CLOSURE & Providing Basic Listening Skills
Police officers Setting The P.A.C.E.

After the critical incident scene is stabilized, **Assess the *Closure* Status** of those involved. The closure status is – how well is each person dealing with what has just happened? You can actually assess this relatively quickly if you know what to look for.

Some Physical Signs of Closure To Watch For Include:

✓ Individuals **Nodding Their Heads** in agreement to a number of concepts, while simultaneously exhibiting:

✓ Several **Exhales of Breath Over 10 minutes** of time or longer (indicating a steady release of tension)

✓ **Body Positions** Turn from a *Closed* stance to an **Open stance**

✓ **Facial Expressions** Appear More **Relieved** and more complacent

© 2014 Mary Kendall Hope

If the Individual(s) You are working with are NOT showing Signs of Closure at first, this is normal. It means that you need to take a few moments and apply some basic listening skills (chapter nine).

2. Listen – Using Basic Listening Skills (Chapter 9)

Ask: "How are you Sir/Maim?" Use you P.A.C. E. skills – 3 C's NO S. Caring, Compassion, Confidence, No Stereotyping. Remember the detail from chapter nine, and use these skills as you **listen for five to ten minutes.** Once you practice your skills, it will not take very long for you to show empathy, clarify, summarize and assess the person's closure status again. A word or two about closure:

Closure

Closure is a vital component of any cathartic event in one's life. This belief stems from the theories of Gestalt theory, popularized in the late 1950's by Fritz Perls (1973). The Gestalt theory presented - that closure is a necessary component of the resolution of conflict. This theory stated that outcome measures of conflicts *that had not reported an adequate reach of "closure"* were less successful than those who did report a "closure," of open issues.

This final process of resolution is just as important as the beginning and middle of the process to the victim. To open a festering wound without properly completing treatment of the infection within, leaves the laceration exposed and vulnerable to even deeper hurt. Just as any wound leaves the area it affects more open to greater harm, so does the opening of a dispute have the potential to more deeply harm those it affects without proper closure. **Re-Assess after about 10 minutes of listening:**

Victims begin to signal that they are at a better position emotionally showing at least 4 – 7 of the following signals:

Ready for Referral to Second Responders

1. **Is Oriented Times 4**: Person, Place, Time, Medical Condition which includes Psychological Condition
   - If an individual is in denial of their psychological needs then take time to talk with them
2. **Shows Confidence in Speaking**
3. Feels able to express and **Receive Both Positive & Negative Feedback** in a respectful manner
4. Able To **Talk About What's Happened Clearly** & In a manner that makes sense – shows perception of reality
5. Able to **Handle Small Disagreements** on the scene
6. **Uses Personal Power Appropriately** – doesn't try to dominate or overpower officers or other victims
   - If individuals are bullying others, take time to talk to them – this is a red flag that this person is experiencing an intense state of crisis & may become violent
7. **Shows Less Anxiety** and/or their anxiety feels manageable

© 2014 Mary Kendall Hope

These non-verbal indicators along with other verbal statements indicate that the disputants have reached a new position in their beliefs about their problems. When this happens, it is a signal to you, a first responder that it is the best time to 3. Make a Referral to this individual to counseling or another second responder professional that can continue to help them.

3. Police officers *Refer* Using 3 C's

If disputants resist their own instincts to reach closure, it may indicate that they have other unresolved issues. Often, these issues are individualistic and apply only peripherally to the dispute in question. In other words, their own internal conflicts may be holding them back from resolving the critical incident– even though the work they have done to resolve it constitutes resolution. In these instances, the first responder must initiate closure and assess the disputants' reactions. State to the person:

"I'm going to refer you to_____ who will give you good supportive help."

As a first responder, you've done your job well. You've gone the distance and taken time to care and secure the link in the chain to the next professional who can surround this person with support and continued help.

Referrals to Counseling

As a first responder, you must focus your skills on the goals of helping these humans survive this critical incident. However, as a human being; you may see a need for this family and recognize how much help another professional could be to them. When you refer individuals and families who have serious problems to other professionals, you give those who come to see you the best service.

When you encounter a member of the public who and realize that this person or family is experiencing significant trauma and reactions to trauma, a gentle reference in private to how a specific counselor you know - could continue to help them is best. Assure not to refer one side (in a domestic violence situation) to counseling while the other side is present.

Refer members of the public to a counseling professional that you have known for some time and trust. If you do not know a good professional counselor, then it is best to refer them to a fellow professional who has a well-established reputation for good service.

4. Follow-Up with Other Agencies Through Your Department's Command Structure

Following up after a critical incident with other agencies is very important to all parties involved. The only time we improve and learn happens when we simply MAKE TIME to discuss it. When departments **MAKE it a Priority and Routine to follow up with other agencies after critical incidents** – First Response to all Future Critical Incidents Improves. If you are part of an agency who already does this ROUTINELY –then you know *why* this is such an important reason your agency is successful.

Not every agency does this. If yours doesn't – START. **Never disregard the importance of small things that happened *differently* – they WILL happen again.** Now the other component of this follow up comes from my own professional experience. I remember long ago seeing a group of children who had allegedly been molested by their father. The first responders were the ones who kept bringing the repeating problem to the attention of all other professionals.

The father in this case was very good at getting around every method of arrest, intervention and prevention, but I as their therapist and I "had his number."(I saw through his lies.) My follow up with police helped save those children in the long run from ongoing sexual abuse. He was eventually arrested and the children protected & given long term care from multiple agencies, thank goodness.

A second example I can think of was a teenager who was threatening to kill people. The other therapists didn't take him seriously. I did. I worked with him for a very long time and he eventually recovered, but at first, his letters - threatening to kill others – I took seriously and coordinated with many support agencies to get him help and protect others from him while he did eventually recover– over a long period of time. His own scars were deep from a severe past. That follow-up saved lives.

Be proactive. I know you must adhere to protocol. I know you must be careful of lawsuits and calls to your city municipal to complain. Mentally ill people do that. Here's my recommendation – coordinate follow up with a <u>good, experienced</u> counselor. They can give you the criteria/ justification you need to intervene. Therapists have to know behavioral qualifiers – it's our job. We don't get paid unless we know how to document behavior correctly.

When you **know** you need to go through your protocols at your department and follow-up – **DO SO**. It does save lives. The first response team will benefit from follow-ups, as victims will thank you many times in silence and also verbally in the community. They will comment on what a good job police officers did.

No, you will not be needed for continued professional service.

You will also not have the professional business time to call every individual you provide critical incident service too, but imagine how much a family who lost a home to fire or home invasion would appreciate a follow up call from the first responder who was there and stayed to refer them to continued help. It would mean so much to them. This caring would go a long way toward empowering these folks in their recovery.

It is uncommon for victims to seek more emergency service over the very *same* issues, but it does happen. When it does, your confidence in setting clear boundaries will take care of this.

What happens more often is individuals speak highly of their local first response team because they have had a good experience with you and appreciate that you cared enough to call them to follow up.

Take time to follow-up when you can. Have a list of referral sources at your ready disposal so that you can refer individuals to someone *else* to help them that you know and trust.

The "On Screen" Hero's: There Because of REAL Police officers

I seldom comment on the quotes I place into the fronts all of the chapters of my books. I like to let the original author's inspiration – (that inspired *me* to place their words there) – to stand on its own merit. For this chapter, Clint Eastwood's real words come from his own knowledge that *if you want something done right, do it yourself.*

Police officers are our real-life "Clint Eastwood's and "John Wayne's." Getting into your vehicles and riding straight into trouble when someone needs help in REAL LIFE takes skill and real courage. These two specific actors were never police officers – but I have found in reading over many of the quotes from their work that they both (as well as many other icons) found inspiration in YOU – the Police, Fire & EMS Professionals who protect and inspire them.

The P.A.C.E. Method – Enhancing Your Own Protocols

You already do such fine, highly skilled work. You save us all – many times without anyone knowing or thanking you for what you've done for them. THANK YOU. Thank you for caring enough to choose this field of work – to accept a basic salary, basic health care package and skinny retirement plan in exchange for giving your life each and every day in sacrifice to others. We are all proud and thankful for you.

Your existing training protocols are exemplary and through continued work, they will continue to better address and assure the safety of the public and your fellow professionals. I hope this P.A.C.E. Method Training will enhance your training with a new simple way of approaching every critical incident you encounter.

Your place on my "RING of Conflict Resolution" is clear. I re-titled the "RING" to one of "First Response" because without YOU – the RING, encircling a cycle of violence does not BEGIN. You BEGIN the chain of help that can surround a cycle of violence with continued help – so that people can transform their lives *out* of the ruts that keep them down and failing.

It's Up to You: SET The P.A.C.E.

When our fellow humans fail, we ALL Fail. **Literally.** When we (any of us) seek any kind of service from a person who is *failing* in their life at home, we all reap the negative benefits. **We all get a *less* healthy, *less* able, and *less* efficient - fellow individual staring back at us**. What happens when you really *need that person or persons* to help YOU?

We must as a society pick up the ball and <u>begin</u> good chains of help – that surround humans and help them to change the cycles of violence they live within. We all can do it.

Police officers ARE the first link in that chain. Set The P.A.C.E. from the first moment you step from your vehicle. Your calm, confident responses delivered with compassion and without stereotype – **BEGIN The P.A.C.E.** Your Consistency and Efficiency come with practice. The *Role-Plays for Resolution II Workbook* will give you scenarios to run through to practice these skills. You can read them and go through *mentally* how you would react as you read and consider the examples separately.

Mental preparation WORKS as a first step toward mastery – but you will need to *role-play* **with others** in-person to reach the consistency and efficiency that will help you to **Maintain The P.A.C.E.** The goal is to P.A.C.E. your responses in the minutes you have at the scene of a critical incident. It's up to you. **Set The P.A.C.E.** I, YOU, Your Co-workers, Your Department and ALL of my fellow humans will benefit from *first response* that is P.A.C.E.D.

Chapter 9

Fellow Professionals on the Scene & Just Afterward. *How Strong is Your Posse?*

In the old west, a posse of *vigilante* police officers went after criminals, arsonists... Today, social media youth refer to a *posse* as a group of people you associate with – some friends, some "associates" or just people who know you or your friends, but you may not trust these posse members as friends.... The same is true in the first responder work environment.

I am *old school*. Friends are people you can count on. Even though that definition has *not* changed – this new concept of a "posse" among young people has a negative connotation – and to me, it sounds like this negative connotation is accurate. This imagery is important to me as a trainer of police officers. You didn't choose your posse. The chief did. But you must work with them well to get the job done.

As a first responder, your co-workers are a vital part of your life. If they aren't, then maybe you're not in the ideal work environment *yet*. Regardless of the quality of the co-workers you work with, they ARE your posse. They go with you as police professionals to get the "bad guys." They pick up a hose or a stretcher with you when an emergency calls for it..

How strong is Your Posse?

This is something you need to assess. Who are the bullies on your posse? Who is young and in need of mentoring? Who is strong and using The P.A.C.E.? Where do *you* fall in this continuum? Maybe *you* are the weakest link...We all go through bad patches in our lives. There is no shame in that. But recognize when you are the bad posse member – or determine whether or not you're going to be a good posse member. How many strong, experienced P.A.C.E. Posse members can you rely on as your real back up and support system?

If you don't have a strong posse, this situation can be remedied if your department goes through a good P.A.C.E. Method training. What about the bullies who are not going to change – you think? Time and influence from stronger P.A.C.E. professionals will change bullies. But right now, assess where your good support system of co-workers reside. You probably already know whom you can count on. You also probably know whom you can go to for help – because they are the most experienced members of your staff.

Think About the Last Time You Worked With A Collection of Fellow Police officers (Consider several past situations)

WHO was In Charge? Was that person capable?

If **YES**:

Did you become a team player immediately? Did you **Empower and Support t**he person in charge and add only positive feedback? If you did – you were **Keeping The P.A.C.E**. This is what a good posse member does. If you didn't, Here's some:

Guidelines When You Have A Good Posse:

1. **Avoid Any Type of Interpersonal Professional Conflict** because the situation is stressful already. *Table It* for Later.
2. **Save "Being Right"** and simply **Suggest Options** at the Scene.

3. **Empower a good leader.** Tell him/her that he/she is right and this *other* option(s) would help him/her resolve the situation.
4. **Work With & Along Side A Each Other As Equals**. Allow the leader to take the credit. Those around you will recognize your input and reward you later and the situation will improve because you worked together as a team.

If **NO**:

Guidelines When You DO NOT Have A Good Posse:

1. The most important thing is to do is help those in crisis in the moment to calmly and safely *stabilize* their situation during a critical incident.

2. Use Your P.A.C.E. Method whenever possible.

3. Do not compete with the Unskilled Leader, continue to follow directives. Seek support from other police officers who are using good leadership skills and

4. Work with the Existing Leader to Resolve the Situation *Well*

If you have the intelligence to recognize a poor leader, then have the courage to address it appropriately. Go to another good leader (a superior you trust). Assure that it is someone you can trust. If there is no one you can trust then rely on your P.A.C.E. and keep doing your best. If this superior is someone you can trust, tell them that you are ***"not coming to them to get someone in trouble or make trouble. You are coming to seek council."*** Talk to them. Ask them what to do.

If you are not in a supportive environment, apply for a different job in another first responder situation that is healthy.

Trouble *Within* the POSSE, But Solvable Issues

If you are experiencing a dispute in a first responder *business setting* then the approach is different. Leave the office politics for the appropriate venue, but still use your P.A.C.E:

P – Prepare Yourself to
A – Act /Speak with
C – Consistency &
E – Efficiency

The P.A.C.E. applies here for a separate but *related* set of reasons. When you face disputes and conflicts in a business setting it feels like a crisis very quickly because of *where* you are experiencing the dispute and because those you experience the dispute/conflict *with* are members of your work life as a first responder – its different. You face crisis OUT THERE. The last thing any co-worker wants to consider in their work building is crisis IN HERE. You must face it anyway. Here are some methods from my ***Negotiate: Resolve it Right Book*** – from the chapter on conflicts in the work setting.

At work when you face a dispute:

❖ **Stop, take a deep breath, and find a reason to take a brief moment *away*** from the situation. *Grab a quick cold beverage or take a moment to visit the restroom*. It will give you and the other person the moment to think and react better.

❖ **Don't Leave & Text someone or Eat**. Don't call anyone or check your messages. This is disrespectful and will inflame the situation. You can take a sip from a beverage; most people would give you a *pass* for this, as it denotes that you're trying to cool down.

In the moments you are away from the situation:

❖ **Push *Your* Reset Button**. Even if you've had an argument with this person before or you are presently in an argument with this person now, don't feel that you have to return to it.

⇒ Think of it as a mistake you made in a marathon of running too fast for a while. When you get that first breather, resolve to reset yourself into a new pace that is going to successfully complete this objective. **The objective is to maintain this working relationship** with a positive conclusion to this particular point or working situation.

These guidelines apply to all conflicts in a work setting. Business conflicts are different because **you do not want to go into your deeper emotional feelings**. It is not the right environment to do this.

In the movies, a great deal of drama and melodrama happens in work place settings. This works in the movies because story lines are designed to represent larger societal motif's to please the audience.

⇒ In real life it is not appropriate to talk about your deeper emotional needs in the work setting. It is best to learn how to ask for what you need respectfully and respond respectfully to others.

Here's where my guidelines differ for police officers. If arguments happen, **De-brief**. I guide others to *let things go*, but as a first responder, if you let it go – it might blow up on you twice as strong later. You need to resolve the conflict with your co-work *right*. If you do not – a crisis or critical incident later will definitely bring the unresolved issues back up.

Do not shove to the back burner – deal with it right. I am including my "how to" guide from my Negotiate book for free for you – to give you a method to resolve it so that it doesn't impede your ability to utilize Your P.A.C.E on the job.

Co-Worker / Co-Worker Disputes

When you have a dispute **with a co-worker or individual who is at the same level** of employment status as you (you're both supervisors, department heads, or on nearly the same status level at your work site) then first accept that you both are equal.

⇒ This person deserves your respect no matter what your feelings are about their personal or professional choices. They likely annoy you and you disagree with a great deal about how they do their job.

Even if you respect this person and you both just disagree on something *still* use this guide.

I've begun the process above with setting your mind on PACE.

**These Steps BELOW Apply in
<u>Any</u> *One on One* Dispute at the Same Level
In An Argument or Before One Starts**

1. Stop & Take a Break
2. Give a good reason – *restroom/ cold beverage*
3. Come back to the situation and Ask **"What do *you* think?" "I really do want to understand your perspective."**
4. Allow them to talk. When/If they ask you the same.

5. Respond by first **complimenting this person on something you *genuinely* like that they did.**

6. Then very simply and succinctly **give them your opposing opinion and offer another option.**
7. **Ask what they think** about the other option
8. If the response is positive, then very slowly enter into **2 -3 more exchanges** if the conversation is positive and

9. **Bring the conversation to a positive close**

10. Back in your own private space or desk, **make note of the positive things that happened** and what you learned. Bring these into your next conversation with this person.

IF THE CONVERSATION GOES BADLY

From either point (#4 on *or* #6 on) from the previous list then say:

1. **"I understand how you came to that conclusion or why you think that."**

2. STOP
3. Do not try and convince the other person that you are right and that they are wrong. **Do not justify your position.** Do not give them a long history of the problem that shows how you are right. Just stop.

4. Pause and nod your head. You're not nodding in agreement **you are nodding that you understand as you listen** and do not interrupt.

5. Consider their perspective. Continue to remain silent or only say one or two words that are positive – indicating that you hear them.
6. If they ask you to respond (*seeming to instigate a fight*) do not take the bait. Just say: **"I am taking a moment to hear you and understand."**

7. **End the conversation well.**
8. You do not have to agree with someone to work with him/her or even like this person. **It may be an issue that can just drop. If it is. Drop it. Move on.**

9. If the problem must be dealt with beyond your disagreement, then very quietly and not in a blaming way, go to your supervisor and very objectively let him/her know that the two of you simply disagree. **Do not make the other person wrong or try and place yourself in a favorable position no matter how much you may think that you need to.** Your HR person &/or Supervisor will see right through you and likely this will hurt your standing with them.

10. It will be much more beneficial to you to **honestly talk to your supervisor** and let them know that **you want to do everything you can to work it out.**

Co-Worker / Supervisor

In these disputes there is **a power imbalance**. The supervisor has power over the employee and therefore the conversation is really not about collaboration. Since **the supervisor has the power to fire you or give you a poor mark on a job performance**, it is up to the employee to **survive** and get through the dispute by respecting the supervisor.

Never fight with a supervisor. If some person is going to be physically harmed then you may step in and prevent harm. If an injustice is happening, then go to the supervisor and pose the discussion this way:

1. **"Thank you for making a few moments to talk with me about___"**
2. Be as brief and specific as you can. The night before or the week before take some time and think carefully about how to **say the least amount of words as possible.**
3. **Use only positive words and phrases.**
4. Present your problem in 1 – 3 sentences.
5. Avoid bringing in any other co-worker into the situation to "make your case stronger" when you are presenting the problem. **Just present this from your perspective only.**
6. Stop. **Listen respectfully** to the response you get. **Do not interrupt**.
7. **Summarize** what they have told you very positively and briefly.
8. Do no rant and rave. Do not go into a long story. If you are asked to tell your story, make the story as brief as possible.
9. Stop.
10. Say, **"I need some time to think on this."**
11. **Thank the supervisor** for their time that they gave you.
12. **Leave the situation positively** and return to work.

If you are dealing with a supervisor who continues to pick and pick, just continue to respectfully say, **"I need to take some time to think on what you've told me to do."**

If your supervisor does not offer you any advisement, then just say **"Thank you for making some time to talk to me. I appreciate your leadership. I will go back to work now and consider how I can make this better on my end."** Use specifics from your work environment.

Bad Bosses

Many supervisors out there don't know how to resolve conflicts. Many don't know how to be supervisors. You must let go of your frustration about this. All you can do is talk to them and talking to them positively is a good step in the right direction.

If you keep what you have to say positive, then when you look back on the conversation, you will be glad you did.

⇒ If you are in a situation that does not resolve itself in a few weeks, then talk to your Human Resources Manager. If you don't have this opportunity then you must think deeply about this situation. **Is it worth risking your job?** Should you look for employment somewhere else?

Consider going to the next level of supervision if you feel it is worth the risk and you must. **Use the exact same guidelines (co-worker/supervisor) with even more respect**.

⇒ Remember to **avoid blaming anyone** and re-state that **you want to do all that you can to help resolve this issue** and **request that the conversation remain confidential**. It may *not* remain confidential, but if you feel it is worth the risk, then do what you need to do to help resolve the problem. You may simultaneously want to look for another place of employment because if the problem persists and is *this* bad then you would want to work in an environment that is not so stressful.

Supervisor / Employee

Any person in a supervisory position between employees below and management above will need to practice conflict resolution skills, because one of your job responsibilities will be to resolve disputes.

If you are a supervisor, likely you are a **Type A** Personality, meaning that you are ambitious and work very hard.

⇒ If you haven't also developed the skills you need to turn off the "high" lever on your work personality let me first encourage you to **find out where you "high" and "low" switches are inside** yourself.

⇒ When an employee comes to talk to you or if you need to go to an employee or management, you will need to **switch your internal work mode to "low." Reset your P.A.C.E**. Prepare yourself to make brief positive statements and to slow down and think before you respond.

Employees are going to come to you in conflict and ask you for answers. **Take some time to formulate your responses.** Take a break and consider what you will say. Cool drinks – always cool down situations: grab both of you one. Feel free to comfort the employee and let them know that you will come back to them tomorrow with more specific steps.

Deliver all steps, responses, statements and directives to an employee with the utmost respect.

Thank the employee for specific aspects of what he/she is doing well.

Keep your word and return to talk to the employee

Keep the conversation private and the fact that the meeting occurred confidential. If you must make notes in a personnel file, then consult your manager or HR director about the best way to do this before writing anything down.

SUPERVISOR/EMPLOYEE
Delivering A Reprimand or Negative Feedback

1. **"Thank you for coming in to talk with me about___"**
2. Be as brief and specific as you can.
3. First tell the employee **how much you appreciate the fine work he/she has done in 1-3 specific areas** _____, _____, _____.
4. Present the problem or issue **in one sentence**. Keep it simple. Do not go into multiple issues. One problem at a time.
5. Ask them how they feel about this. Give them plenty of time to respond. Encourage them to tell you their side. **Listen respectfully** to the response you get. **Do not interrupt.**
6. **Summarize** what they have told you very positively and briefly.
7. **Ask them if they have any suggestions.**
8. Listen carefully. You may learn something very valuable from this employee. **Employees often have problems with variables that may need *address* from higher management.**

9. Say **"Thank you for the feedback you gave me. I will consider this."**
10. Give the directive(s) you need to positively and briefly.

11. Ask, **"Do you have any questions?"** Answer these questions clearly and specifically. Take time to clear up very small details with patience.

12. Ask, **"Do you understand what needs to happen next?"**
13. Summarize positively what you've gone over and **emphasize the employee's strengths. Let them know you believe in their ability.**

14. Leave the situation positively and return to work.
15. Remember, resolutions are built like a brick foundation. Lay one solid brick at a time. **If you have a good conversation with an employee it can begin a new experience for them at work.**

❖ Foster a good work atmosphere by bringing snacks for everyone and whenever you can, **work along side employees.** This gives you a good chance to show your leadership abilities when the opportunity arises.

The best way to avoid reprimanding employees is **to check in positively with them often.** Talk to them and reward them for doing well.

Chapter 10

If you want to be successful, it's just this simple. Know what you are doing.
Love what you are doing. And believe in what you are doing.

Will Rogers

MEDIATION Techniques & Listening Skills
For *Police officers* – This Chapter Will Help You in the *5 Minutes* You Have

"We Could Use Some of Those Mediation Skills Around <u>Here</u>"

I am including this chapter for Police officers because every time I tell a first responder what I do for a living TODAY – (I teach mediation). I get the same response: ***"I could use some of those mediation skills...."***

Well, I'm <u>not</u> going to try and train you to be mediators.

Police officers DO need good mediation skills every day when they are faced with two people who are arguing. How often are you in situations like that? Daily? Periodically throughout your workweek? I'd be willing to bet that as a first responder, you face individuals in conflict with one another constantly.

FIRST Allow Me To Ground This Discussion

I'm assuming that you get some mediation skill training in your *own* certification programs – so what I have to share with you is some simplified instructions to supplement your existing training as well as some excerpts from a text book I originally wrote in 2009 that is used in community colleges and universities.

This chapter will give you a little deeper background on *where* (those you want to mediate *with*) – may be coming from. As a second responder, we are trained to *"meet them where they're at"* instead of "tell them where they should be." This is the major differences between a first and second responder. Police officers direct individuals – to where they need to go. Second responders take them from there forward – allowing each individual we work with - to set their own PACE.

This mediation background will help you to develop your skills, so that when you get the chance to say the one or two lines you have time to say, those sentences will be better – because you've read *this* and began to think through the skills of mediating.

Ask me do I know how to use the **one sentence** (I can get in edgewise) with a person in crisis *well*. Yes, I learned this through **fire** *myself.* As a *second* responder, my job was first to listen. Individuals in crisis – who finally have a forum – TALK. So, through years of time, I learned that the best thing for me to do was to not interrupt and let them get their emotions off their chest in a safe place where someone listening cared. When *you*, a first responder are faced with two individuals or more who are fighting, assume my second responder role for just a few moments:

Listen first. Then, listen some more. **When you get a chance to respond, choose your words carefully, kindly, and positively**. This is still one of the best skills I can teach you. **When you do not know what else to do, listen.** Ask a simple question of discovery (when, who, what) then stop and listen. Don't feel awkward in the silence. Allow the silence to heal. Sometimes, the best thing to do is just listen. This will often de-escalate the situation faster than anything else. What people do not have today are people who will listen and take time with them. Give them what they need most.

MEDIATION SKILLS:

Here's one of the cardinal rules of both counseling and mediation: *Meet them Where They're At*. Don't try and tell them what to do or change them. Accept them as is. One of the best first skills to learn – that permeates the entire mediation or negotiation process is empathy.

Stepping Into the Disputants' Shoes

Recall first an experience that you have had when someone listened to you, but it was obvious that they cared very little about your feelings. Possibly, we all are able to call up any number of instant memories in a variety of situations in which others appear to listen to us, but do not show us that they completely understand, empathize, or identify with what we (in that moment) are experiencing.

I will define some terms of listening in this chapter, but it is important to first distinguish how a person who is not listened to *feels*. To truly help the disputants (a **disputant** is an individual in conflict) you must imagine

how it felt to "walk in their shoes." To understand what each side is feeling is a good definition of **empathy**. Showing empathy while you listen will help you respond with kindness. As a mediator, the ability to show kindness goes a long way toward stimulating the disputants to work together collaboratively.

One of the best ways a mediator can learn to empathize is to envision *himself* in similar situations to the disputant. The disputants' situation and feelings will be different, but it is a helpful exercise.

***Your* Experiences With Empathy**

Imagine a recent experience in a "drive-thru" food restaurant in which you had a question about something or a specific need for your "order." How did the service person treat you? Did you feel understood, cared about, or appreciated? Compare the feelings you imagined with how a *caller* might feel when making first contact with your mediation office.

Now imagine taking back an item to a department store. You do not have your receipt and must explain why. Did the person take the time to understand your situation? How did you feel when they did (or did not understand)? Compare this to how a potential mediation client may feel if they have told you something that was hard to explain in an initial conversation.

Finally, imagine that you must reveal the most embarrassing collection of information about yourself to a perfect stranger and simultaneously ask for his help. How do you feel? Are you scared? What will the stranger say? Will he judge you? How will you defend your mistakes? The comparison here is obvious. An individual *you* help will experience all of the feelings and questions above before, during, and after his time spent with you in mediation.

Your Reponses As a First Responder – Mediating A Dispute

How will *you* respond? Will you take the time to understand disputants' worst mistakes from *their* perspective? How will you gently and patiently confront them on the things they did wrong? Will you expect the conversation to get emotional, difficult, confusing, embarrassing, and awkward? It will.

If you deliver kind, caring, and empathetic responses to your disputants, you can expect the conversation to get emotional and awkward. This (to me) is a good sign that you are doing your job well. You will be one-step further toward a better reaction to difficult statements if you go *in* (to the listening/responding experience) expecting the road to be rocky before it gets smooth. No one can ever react perfectly to every situation posed him in the exact moment it is posed.

It "counts" if you recognize a *reaction mistake* and correct it the next time you have an opportunity. A **reaction mistake** is measured in the <u>response from the disputant</u>. If the disputant's face becomes pained or he voices disapproval or disagreement with your reaction, you may then assess that you need to react in a kinder manner to this topic. It is likely that the topic is causing him more pain than you anticipated. Take a moment and gently ask if you understood; this should clear the misunderstanding.

It matters if you are patient and kind. It is all right to ask questions gently and with caring. Image that it is *you* that is telling the same tale that you are hearing. No one can completely know how another expects to be responded to in order to feel understood, but we can *all* convey kindness and understanding.

This is what every disputant will expect of you. As a first responder who is mediating *your* ego must go "out the window" in sacrifice of their need for someone to understand, to care, and to share with them for a little while – their pain, disappointment, anger, embarrassment, guilt, and sadness. Do your best. If you fail, begin again.

Use Your MOLERS – Basic LISTENING Technique for Police officers

Use Your MOLERS – Basic Listening
The Foundation of Good Conversation

M - **maintain respectful eye** contact
O - **open** your posture & your mind
L - **LISTEN** without interruption
E - respond with **empathy** and
R - **refer individuals** for continued help
S – without **stereotyping**

© 2014 Mary Kendall Hope

Your mol<u>ar</u>s (in your mouth) are your back teeth. Let their imagery guide your listening. **PLACE THEM TOGETHER More Often and *Use Your MIND and Your Ears*** and this MOLERS (with an E) technique. It works.

Two More Essential Listening Skills

1. **Focus solely on what the speaker is saying.** Try not to think about what you are going to say next. The conversation will follow a logical flow after the speaker makes his point…
2. **Minimize internal distractions.** If your own thoughts keep horning in, simply let them go and continuously refocus your attention on the speaker."

Eye Contact

Looking individuals in the eye with a kind expression conveys instantly that the speaker has your attention. As a mediator, you need to maintain eye contact, to the degree that you and the disputants are comfortable. If the disputants appear to feel uncomfortable with constant eye contact, then periodically focus on areas close to their face, but *away* from direct eye contact.

Stay focused on each disputant's facial area throughout the mediation process and do make direct eye contact in a kind manner periodically throughout mediation. A mediation between two parties is a business transaction as well as a session of listening; the disputants need their professional to keep them focused on the business at hand. Their objective is to reach an equitable agreement that respects them both if at all possible.

Facial Expression

As a *first responder* who is mediating a dispute, your facial expressions need to reflect a degree of emotion. Do not let your face remain stoic in reaction to extremely volatile information – good or bad. Show the disputants with your facial expression that you are listening. In a very genuine manner, listen to the stories disputants tell you and let your eyes, eyebrows, mouth, and entire face reflect that you are listening. You do not need to be overdramatic to convey that you are genuinely interested in what they need to tell you.

Posture

Your posture very clearly reflects whether your facial expressions are indeed genuine. A professional who is listening shows very clear body posturing – moving his body *toward* the speaker. **Face the person speaking.** Lean forward slightly to show you are paying attention.

You may also show your attention by turning both shoulders/ upper body toward the speaker while you are working at a dry-erase board, laptop or other tool of mediation. Even if you have to turn away, be aware of your body when you do so and be aware that you are turned away while you are writing or collecting material.

Remember to turn back and refocus immediately on the speaker in a kind manner as soon as you are able. The speaker will unconsciously be aware that you did this and will further unconsciously appreciate this gesture.

Eighty Percent of Communication is NON-VERBAL
Here Are Some Body Posturing Techniques That Will Help You in Every Aspect of Your Job As A First Responder:

Open & Closed Body Positions

An **open** body position indicates that a person is emotionally "open" or receptive to new ideas and information. Open body positions look "open." Arms and legs are open (not crossed) and a person's body is often turned toward the person speaking. Facial expressions reflect more open or upward brows and more receptive mouth position (nearer to a smile). Open body positions further indicate that the listener is "open" to new concepts. It notes to the speaker *unconsciously* that the listener will accept was he has to say.

A **closed** body position indicates that a person is emotionally "closed" to receiving new information and ideas. Closed body positions likewise, look "closed." Arms and legs are usually crossed and a person's body is turned away from the person speaking.. Facial expressions reflect downwardly cast brows and a less receptive mouth position (nearer to a frown). Sometimes, arms or legs (one or the other set) are not crossed, but the body overall reflects disagreement and a "positioning" away from the person speaking. Closed body positions further indicate that the listener is "closed" *figuratively* to new concepts. It notes to the speaker unconsciously that the listener will not accept was he has to say.

Mirroring

While you are seated and listening to the person speaking, assure that you very slowly begin to mirror their body movements. **Mirroring** is the act of imitating body movements, as if looking at the person (speaking) in a mirror.

Your movements of body (as the first responder) should be a "mirror" reflection of the other person. You will find that if you begin to pay attention to yourself, you may realize that you are automatically mirroring others without realizing this. After any professional practices this movement for a while, they will begin to do this instinctively.

It is important to pay attention to your body's movements and mirror the person who is speaking. When you mirror a speaker, you let them know non-verbally, that you are "with" them – or that you understand them and are "on their side." Disputants need this; they are describing emotional problems, and they need non-verbal affirmation as well as verbal support that the professional involved cares.

Do not Judge or Give Advisement

The biggest pitfall a professional can make is giving advisement to disputants on how to solve the problems brought to mediation. I have seen new mediators write website blogs about how to give advice to disputants in mediation. In my experience, giving advice is a mistake.

Effective mediation helps people to solve their own problems, which is more effective than any advice given. Careful too that you do not begin to judge disputants' problems without recognizing this behavior in yourself.

Assure that as soon as the urge to judge or advice arises in you, you become aware of this feeling and refocus your listening skills and responses in a neutral and empathetic understanding. **To quote an old joke: When you feel the urge to give advice, lie down until the feeling passes.**

To keep the conversation flowing:

Say phrases such as:

"*I wasn't aware of that," Tell me more...*" [with genuine intention].

You may also use prompts that are more direct:

"*What did you do then?*" and "*What did she actually do?*"

Conveying Empathy & Compassion

Conveying *empathy* is one of the most challenging components of active listening, yet without it, a disputant will not feel listened to. Likewise, to convey a sense of authentic *compassion* (to both parties equally) reflects the founding principles of mediation.

Empathy is a feeling of mutual understanding of emotion *and* experience. It is also the ability to communicate understanding. By definition, a situation that requires *empathy* to understand is one in which difficulty has been experienced. **Individuals in dispute are in need of empathy from the moment they call you on the phone to request help.** Think back to our section on "walking in the other person's shoes."

We all need others to empathize with us, even in the simplest situations. Though we may not verbalize it, we all need empathy and well all seek empathy. Often, our need of empathy is unconscious, but when we experience empathy from someone, it is always a welcome occurrence. When humans are in conflict, they both need and expect empathy from others. The problem is they seldom get empathy from others and this intensifies conflict.

The Expectation of Empathy

If disputants do not get empathy, they leave the process, either physically (by not returning to talk -) or emotionally by "checking out". They will cease to challenge themselves to open their minds and not allow themselves to become vulnerable so they may consider new alternatives. What may be their next choice? Violence. Individuals a first responder comes into contact with have been in some way involved in a critical incident. Frustration at not being understood or cared about often leads humans to feel desperate and violence becomes as easy to justify to themselves as an option – as fast food stop when someone feels the survival need to eat.

To stimulate the opposing party to truly imagine the ***other side's experience*** and empathize with how the other side feels *begins* a process of *transformation* within the disputants. These moments, began with a first responder build on one another and will help the individual on a path toward transformation – as time goes on and he or she is exposed to good continued professional help from second and third responders.

Compassion

Showing **compassion** means to reflect in your facial expressions, verbal statements, and body posturing that you care about the difficult situation that is being described to you by the speaker. In showing these behaviors mentioned above, your statements should agree with the speaker's statements and not point out the opposite view point.

For instance, if the speaker states, "I hate it when someone yells at me in traffic for not going fast enough; it stresses me out." A compassionate first responder statement could be, *"**I know; I hate that too.**"* A non-compassionate response would be, *"You shouldn't feel stressed out; you should ignore them."* DO NOT Tell people they "shouldn't" feel the way they feel. This latter statement negates the initial feeling expressed by the speaker and does not convey compassion.

As a first responder, when you convey compassion, you free the disputant to discover his *own* lessons and view points that apply to his situation. You further create an atmosphere of empowerment that will enable the disputant to work through his own obstacles after completing mediation.

Active versus Passive Listening

A distinction between "active" listening and "passive" listening is necessary for the attainment of active listening skills, as these definitions guide the delivery of listening technique. **Passive listening** occurs when one individual (the 1st person) is *present* when someone else (the 2nd person) is talking, but there is no *evidence* that the 1st person (passive listener) is listening.

An example of passive listening occurs in a conversation in an automobile. The 1st person is driving a car and speaking while the passenger (2nd person) sits motionless. The second person in the above scenario is exhibiting passive listening. In this actual situation, it is difficult to *show* active listening, but the <u>physical appearance of the passenger reflects the exact same body posturing and lack of responses</u> that a passive listener shows.

Active listening occurs when one individual (1st person) shows through his behavior that he is listening to the other individual (2nd person). The first person makes eye contact, nods, and asks specific questions that indicate that he (1st person) is actively listening to the other person (2nd person).

Clarifying to Help An Emotional Person Realize the BIG Picture

To clarify points made by a disputant, the first responder asks very specific questions of the speaker. The goal is to move the speaker from a broad generalization to a specific point you can work with.

For example, the disputant states, *I was so mad when he told me about it that I screamed at my child. I probably doomed our daughter to counseling in later life.* The first responder would clarify by slowly asking any one of the following questions:

- ✓ "Let me see if I understand what you were mad about, she didn't come in last night. You didn't see her till today? **Yes**

- ✓ Was she with the inner city gang you mentioned? **Yes**
- ✓ Did you talk to her about it? **Yes**
- ✓ When did that conversation occur? **Yesterday**
- ✓ Have you talked with her since?" **No**

As a first responder, you know how to do this. The same skill set you use to interview a member of the public also helps you to close down a person who is becoming upset. Take that opportunity to gather facts. Clarifying helps a disputant to begin to see the larger problem. He/She also begins to realize that this problem has workable parts that can be improved.

Utilize closed questions and limit open-ended questions when clarifying to keep clients focused on understanding the issues. Slow gentle questioning assists disputants to begin to compartmentalize issues of confusion into issues that they can continue to work on these issues later.

Summarizing

Summarizing what a speaker is saying keeps both you and the speaker "on the same page." To **summarize**, the listener restates everything that he has heard using as many of the exact words and phrases that the speaker used as possible. In pure summarization, the listener would refrain from using their own words and interpretations of what the listener as heard .

A listener should summarize what he has heard after every five to ten sentences, depending on the *gravity* of the information (how heavily filled with emotion) and *intensity* of the information (how much detailed information is in one sentence.

Creating this safe place of focus and supportive attention to the speaker's needs greatly helps an emotional speaker to become calmer and feel more empowered. **Empowerment** enables the speaker to feel as if he has the ability to not only talk about this conflict, but also find resolution.

Confrontation

To **confront** a speaker, the listener challenges what has been said by questioning the accuracy of the speaker's opinions. Confrontation is a difficult process for every first responder; for it places into question the first responder's loyalty (from the disputant's perspective) and neutrality.

Confrontation is best started in the middle of the mediation process. To confront disputants at the beginning of the mediation will damage the rapport between the mediator and both disputants. The **rapport** is the state of trust between the mediator and disputants. A good rapport needs to be well established and maintained throughout any instance of confrontation.

Emotional Healing: Mediation versus Counseling

A prolonged discussion of emotional content is not appropriate for the mediating a dispute. In mediation – the objective is to stimulate disputants to find a resolution to one or two interrelated problems and help the parties reach an agreement that they can maintain over time.

Conflicts strike deep at the heart of what is most precious to us, and conflicts challenge us within an inch of our tolerance. This is what defines the problems that face us in our lives as a "conflict."

The problems what would come to a First Responder (by their very definition) have no solutions readily apparent, and require new, untested pathways to be forged from the deep "forests" of tradition, habit, familiarity, comfort, and unknown territories that exist in our lives.

Our most basic patterns of survival have to be re-written to overcome most conflicts. These prospects are daunting, and those coming to us for help are afraid of taking steps into unknown territory.

The "Can't Do *That*" Syndrome

Disputants have a very great fear of traversing into unknown territory. They tell themselves that they "can't change this" or "won't do it," and subsequently, they cannot do it.

Until an individual gets to a place in his own frame of mind that allows him to empower himself, he actually cannot change. He has imprisoned his own self in handcuffs in his mind – preventing himself from even considering what a "change" could look like – and dooming his next set of interactions to the I "can't do *that*" syndrome.

Pride is an ugly obstacle that a first responder can easily recognize, but a disputant finds invisible. Pride tends to be the most common cause and persistent obstacle of the "I can't do that," syndrome. Take heart, disputants remember the suggestions made.

Give them time to consider what was suggested. Allow them to bring it up again. Listen. Allow them to change their mind without "losing face." (See saving face below) When you allow disputants the respect of declaring that they "can't do that", you give them the freedom to consider how this *could* be possible. They may or may *not* change their mind later, but they are likely to consider other options if they stay engaged in the mediation.

Saving Face, Saving Grace – A Turning Point

Referring a disputant to counseling must be done in complete privacy. Saving face is one of the most important aspects of preserving the power balance in mediation. Assuring that the discussion is "equitable" is one of your most important tasks as a mediator.

The mediation a first responder gives is focused solely on assisting disputants in the resolution of a very specific set of problems – at a very *specific* time in their life. Good mediation focuses disputants on <u>one</u> or <u>two</u> well-defined problems. To resolve one problem well, can be a disputant's turning point. It allows him or her to build a foundation for the successful resolution of other problems within their dispute and indeed within their lives.

Appendix

The P.A.C.E. Method Condensed
P.A.C.E. Forms & Tables

Use Your MOLERS – Basic Listening
The Foundation of Good Conversation

M - **maintain respectful eye** contact
O - **open** your posture & your mind
L - **LISTEN** without interruption
E - respond with **empathy** and
R - **refer individuals** for continued help
S – without **stereotyping**

© 2014 Mary Kendall Hope

The P.A.C.E. Method Condensed

P - PREPARE (to)

The best **Preparation** is the key to completing any task well. The more overwhelming the task, the more important preparation is to success.

<u>Four essential components of good preparation for a first responder:</u>

1. **Complete** your own certification/credentialing training with the **very best** of your own ability.
2. **The P.A.C.E. Method Training** will prepare you to better address members of the public in crisis/conflict situations
3. **PRACTICE** – Complete Role-Plays to Hone Your Knowledge & Ability to Deliver in 5-15 Minutes
4. **Recharge Your Batteries Daily** (Stress Relief), **Weekly** (Weekend Rest), **Quarterly** (Get Away's), **Yearly** (Vacation)

A – ACT (& Speak with)

The next four priorities to guide your professional ACTions are listed in order of use. I will **begin with number four and number one** because number one – prioritizing your game plan begins with HOW you will deliver it.

1. **Prioritize Your Game Plan** for Help and Follow-up
2. Give Yourself **15 Minutes More** & Other Professionals 30
3. **Assure You Know** Before You Speak
4. Deliver Actions With **The 3 C's Confidence, Calm, and Compassion.** Avoid the S & S – Stereotyping & Stigma

C- CONSISTENCY (and)

1. **Turn on Your Professionalism Daily**
2. Bad Day – Take 5 To Re-Set
3. Share only brief positive stories with members of the public
4. Homework- Find your **Compassionate** "Game Face" & positive attitude and put it on every day & every time like your second invisible shirt.

E - EFFICIENCY

Efficiency comes from both continued accurate knowledge and practice. ***De-brief*** after a critical incident that involved multiple deaths, injuries or extreme traumas to both members of the public & police officers.

1. **Sharpen the Blade** –if your department isn't taking time to Debrief, or do Role-Plays to stay fresh – SUGGEST IT.
2. **Re-write the script.** Even if you've done it wrong a hundred times. STOP. Do it right from now on. Re-write and rememorize a NEW script. A better way will be better for YOU, Your Department, The public, and the profession. Use the same compassion each time & adapt as needed for each crisis.
3. **Efficiency comes with practice.** There is no such thing as a short cut to efficiency for police officers.

ON THE SCENE Pocket LIST™
(Maintain the P.A.C.E)

REFFERAL SOURCE	NAME(S)	PHONE
Counselors	_____	_____
Suicide or Other Hotline	_____	_____
Domestic Violence	_____	_____
Social Outreach Programs	_____	_____
Medical Clinic	_____	_____
Homeless Shelter	_____	_____
Food Pantry	_____	_____
Community Program	_____	_____
Red Cross	_____	_____
Salvation Army	_____	_____
OTHER	_____	_____

Use Your 7 STEPS to P.A.C.E.

1. LISTEN w/Respect & Empathy
2. Don't "SHOULD" On Them
3. NO Quick FIX
4. "I can understand how you could feel that way."
5. Don't Interrupt
6. POCKET List
7. Close the Situation Positively

Cycle of Violence

First Responders
Vital LINKS In the Chain of Response

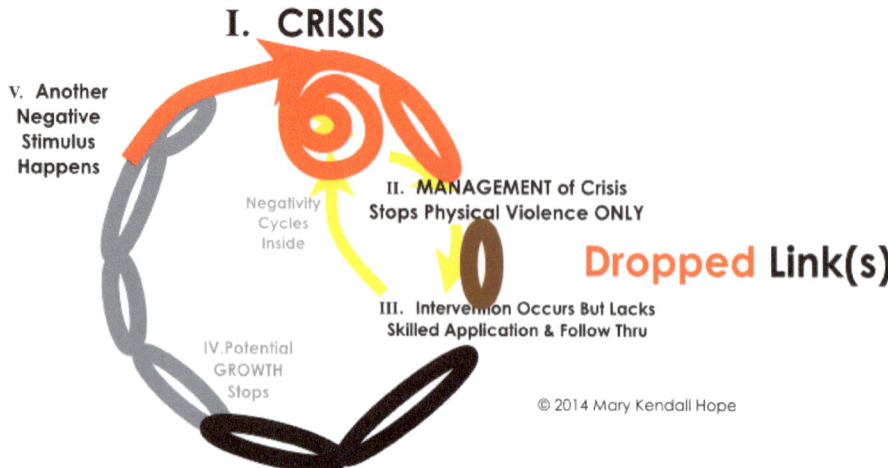

I. CRISIS

V. Another Negative Stimulus Happens

Negativity Cycles Inside

II. MANAGEMENT of Crisis Stops Physical Violence ONLY

Dropped Link(s)

IV. Potential GROWTH Stops

III. Intervention Occurs But Lacks Skilled Application & Follow Thru

© 2014 Mary Kendall Hope

RING of *First* Response
Replacing The LINKS

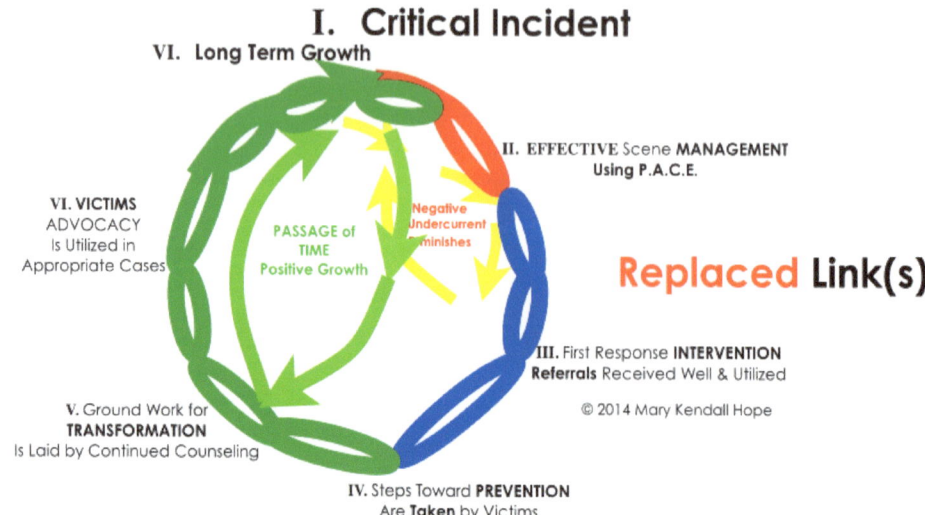

I. Critical Incident

VI. Long Term Growth

II. EFFECTIVE Scene MANAGEMENT Using P.A.C.E.

VI. VICTIMS ADVOCACY Is Utilized in Appropriate Cases

PASSAGE of TIME Positive Growth

Negative Undercurrent Diminishes

Replaced Link(s)

III. First Response **INTERVENTION** Referrals Received Well & Utilized

© 2014 Mary Kendall Hope

V. Ground Work for TRANSFORMATION Is Laid by Continued Counseling

IV. Steps Toward **PREVENTION** Are **Taken** by Victims

References

American Bar Foundation. Retrieved May 20, 2004, from http://web.lexis-nexis.com/universe .

Breslin, J., & Rubin, J. (eds.). (1999). *Negotiation theory and practice*. Cambridge, Massachusetts: The Program on Negotiation at Harvard Law School.

Bush & Folger (2005). *The promise of mediation*: *the transformative model for conflict resolution*. New York: John Wiley & Sons.

Bush, R., & Folger, J. (1994). *The promise of mediation: responding to conflict through empowerment and recognition*. San Francisco, California: Jossey-Bass Publishers.

Doyle, M. & Straus, D. (1976). *How to make meetings work: the new interaction method*. New York: Penguin Putnam

Duchan, J., & Black, M. (2001). "Progressing toward life goals: a person-centered approach to evaluating life therapy." Topics in Language Disorders, v22 n1 p37-49 Nov 2001.

Fisher, R., Ury, W., & Patton, B. (2011, 1991, 1983, 1981). *Getting to yes; negotiating agreement without giving in*. New York: Penguin Books.http://www.nursing.uiowa.edu/sites/chronicwound/Debride1.htm

Gerencser, A. (1995). Family mediation: screening for domestic abuse. *Florida State University Law Review, 23,* p. 43.

Habershon, A. & Garbiel, C. (1907). "Will The Circle Be Unbroken," Song Lyrics. *Alexander's Gospel Songs No. 2.,* p. 33. New York: Fleming H. Revell Company

Hart, T. (1980). *The art of Christian listening*. Mahwah, NJ: Paulist Press.

Hendricks, J.E., McKean, J.B., & Hendricks, C.G. (2010). *Crisis intervention: fourth edition*. Springfield, IL: Charles C. Thomas Publisher

Hippocratic Oath. (2008, July 18). Retrieved July 18, 2008, from http://members.tripod.com/nktiuro/hippocra.htm

Hope, M. K. (2014). *Negotiate: resolve it right*. Raleigh, NC: Pax Pugna Publications.

Hope, M.K. (2006). "Judging mediation: an assessment of the effectiveness of mediation programs in North Carolina," Published Dissertation on Disc. South Bend, IN: Graduate Theological Foundation.

Ivey, A., Gluckstern, N., & Bradford, M. (1982). Basic attending skills. Hanover, MA: Microtraining Associates Incorporated.

June, L., & Black, S. (2002). *Counseling in African-American communities: Biblical perspectives on tough issues*. Grand Rapids, MI: Zondervan.

Justice, T., & Jamieson, D. (1999). *The facilitator's field book*. New York: AMACOM.

Kirchner, M. (2000). "Gestalt therapy theory: An Overview," Gestalt Global Corporation. Vol.4 No. 3. Retrieved 9-2-08 from: http://www.g-gej.org/4-3/theoryoverview.html

Knights, W. (2002). *Pastoral counseling: a gestalt approach*. New York: Routledge.

Kolb, D., & Williams, J. (2000). *The shadow negotiation*. New York: Simon & Schuster.

Kreisberg, L. (2006; 2002; 1998). *Constructive conflicts: from escalation to resolution*. Lanham, Maryland: Rowman & Littlefield Publishers.

Lederach, J.P. (2005). *The moral imagination: the art and soul of building peace.* New York: Oxford University Press.

Listening Skills. (2008, September 4). Retrieved September 4, 2008, from http://www.taft.cc.ca.us/lrc/class/assignments/actlisten.html

LOC. (2008, July 10). Library of Congress Prints & Photographs. Retrieved July 10, 2008, from http://www.loc.gov/rr/print/catalog.html

National Victims Advocacy. (2008, July 14). Retrieved July 14, 2008, from: http://www.trynova.org/

No Harm. (2008, July 18). Retrieved July 18, 2008, from: http://www.geocities.com/everwild7/noharm.html

North Carolina Mediation. (2008, July 7). Retrieved July 27, 2008, from: http://www.nccourts.org/Courts/CRS/Councils/DRC/Default.asp

Passive Active Listening. (2008, September 4). Retrieved September 4, 2008, from: http://www.learncustomerserviceonline.com/Preview/ActiveListeningCS/FrameMaster1.htm

Peck, M.S. (2003;1988). *The road less traveled: timeless edition. a new psychology of love, traditional values and spiritual growth.* New York: Simon & Schuster-Touchstone.

Peck, M. S. (1998). *Farther along the road less traveled: second edition.* New York: Simon & Schuster-Touchstone.

Perls, F. (1973). *The gestalt approach and eyewitness to therapy.* Palo Alto, CA: Science & Behavior Books, Incorporated.

Rogers, C. (1959). "A theory of therapy, personality and interpersonal relationships, as developed in the client-centered framework." In S. Koch (ed.). *Psychology: A study of science. (pp. 184-256).* N.Y.: McGraw Hill.

Schwarz, R. (2002; 1994). *The skilled facilitator: practical wisedom for developing effective groups.* San Francisco: Jossey-Bass Publishers.

Shotwell, V., & Shotwell, R., (2008). *Thinking outside the box: life lessons learned from miracles with meanings.* New York: Wordclay.

Siegal, M., (2008). "First, do no harm." New York Post, June 22, 2008. Retrieved 7-18-08 from: http://www.nypost.com/seven/06222008/postopinion/postopbooks/first__do_no_harm_116584.htm

Slatkin, A. (2009). *Training strategies for crisis and hostage negotiations: scenario writing and creative variations for role-play.* Springfield, IL: Charles C. Thomas Publisher

Strentz, T. (2013). *Hostage/crisis negotiations: lessons learned from the BAD, the MAD, and the SAD.* Springfield, IL: Charles C. Thomas Publisher

Stringer, T. (2004). "Storytelling in mediation: the hero's journey," Retrieved 8-9-08 from: http://www.mediate.com/articles/stringerT.cfm

Tannen, D. (1986). *That's not what I meant: how conversational style makes or breaks relationships.* New York: Ballentine Books.

Ury, W., Brett, J., & Goldberg, S. (1993). *Getting disputes resolved: designing systems to cut the costs of conflict.* Cambridge, Massachusetts: The Program on Negotiation at Harvard Law School

Ury, W. (1993,1991). *Getting past no: negotiating in difficult situations.* New York: Penguin Books.

Umbriet, M. (2006, 1995). *Mediating interpersonal conflicts: a pathway to peace.* West Concord, MN: CPI Publishing.

Wilmot, W., & Hocker, J. (2001). *Interpersonal conflict.* New York: McGraw Hill Publishers.

Wright, H. N. (2003). *Helping those who hurt: how to be there for your friends in need.* Minneapolis: Bethany House.